BEYOND HIS
PASSION

BEYOND HIS
PASSION

The Whole Story of
Jesus Christ's
Death and Resurrection

As Recorded in the Gospels and the
Significance in Time and Eternity

JIM & ROY GILLEY

world
PUBLISHING
SINCE 1928

SOME SPECIFICS ABOUT THIS WORK

The New King James Version translation, copyright by Thomas
Nelson, Inc., Nashville, TN, was used as the basic text in arranging
Beyond His Passion. Word changes to that text are in brackets for
clarity. Some of the readings are a blending of passages from more
than one Gospel. Comments are located occasionally in the text to
provide further information. Verse numbers are not included
because of the blending of readings, and repetitive wording in excess
of that needed for clarity may be eliminated in some readings. A
complete listing of Scripture passages used in arranging *Beyond His
Passion* is located at the end of this work.

We appreciate the contributions received by A.T. Robertson's work, *A
Harmony of the Gospels for Students of the Life of Christ* (New York:
Harper & Brothers, 1922, 1950) and John Franklin Carter's work, *A
Layman's Harmony of the Gospels* (Nashville: Broadman Press, 1961).
An *Interlinear Greek-English New Testament* was also used in writing
this work (Third Edition, Jay P. Green, editor, 1996, Baker Book,
Grand Rapids). Other translations were also reviewed: *The Authorized
King James Version*; *The New International Version*, copyright by
Zondervan Publishing House; *The New Living Translation,* copyright
by Tyndale House Publishers, Inc., Wheaton, Illinois; *The New
American Standard Bible*, copyright by The Lockman Foundation;
The New Revised Standard Version of the Bible, copyright by the
Division of Christian Education of the National Council of the
Churches of Christ in the USA. All used by permission.

WORLD PUBLISHING
Nashville, TN 37214
www.worldpublishing.com

ISBN 0-529-11953-6

Printed in the United States of America

04 05 06 07 08 — 5 4 3 2 1

CONTENTS

INTRODUCTION

THE PASSION OF JESUS was not something which occurred due to fate or man's ability to plan such a horrible event. Instead, it was an event arranged by God and His Son Jesus Christ before the beginning of time. The Bible says that Jesus was the "Lamb slain from the foundation of the world" (Revelation 13:8).

Because Adam rebelled against God at the bidding of Satan (Genesis 3), there was a wall built between God and people. But men and women are God's prize creation. And because of His great love for them, He provided a way to forgive them while retaining His just and righteous character. A way was made to provide men and women the righteousness required to be with God again. In the Garden of Eden, God promised that His Son would come to crush Satan. However, He also stated that His Son would be wounded and bruised as He provided a way back to Him (Genesis 3:14–15). Yes, His Son would suffer, not for His sins, but for the sins of those whom He would bring back to God.

Many people are familiar with John 3:16 which says, "For God so loved the world that He gave His only begotten Son, that whoever believes in Him should not perish, but have everlasting life." But we must understand and accept how John 3:16 can be realized. We must understand that "God made Jesus who knew no sin *to be* sin for us, that we might become the righteousness of God in Him" (2 Corinthians 5:21).

Beyond His Passion is the full account of Jesus' sacrifice, but the story continues with His resurrection from the dead and His ascension to the Father. To gain a full understanding of these accounts, we will begin with the prophecy of His Passion as recorded by Isaiah over 700 years before Jesus was born—in most vivid detail!

THE PASSION
IN PROPHECY

A READING OF PROPHECY RETOLD
AS A HISTORY LESSON

WHO HAS BELIEVED our report? To whom will Jehovah's saving power (arm) be revealed?

For [Jesus] grows up before (Jehovah) like a tender plant, as a root out of dry ground. He has no [special] form to which we should be attracted. Why should we desire Him?

He is despised and abandoned by men. *He is* a Man of pains, acquainted with grief. We hid our faces from Him. Since He was despised, we did not value Him.

But truly, He carried our griefs and pain. We thought He was plagued, stricken, and afflicted by God, but He was wounded for our transgressions *and* bruised for our iniquities. His whipping was for our peace, and with His wounds we were healed.

We *have* strayed like sheep, going our own way, away from God. And Jehovah made Him pay for the iniquity of everyone. He was oppressed and He was afflicted, but did not open His mouth. He was led as a lamb to slaughter. And as a sheep is silent before the shearers, He did not open His mouth. He was *captured*, restrained and denied justice. And who considered His inheritance? *No one!* He was cut off from the land of life by the sinfulness of His own people. *Yes*, the striking went to [Jesus]. His grave was to be with the wicked, but at His death, He was in the grave of a rich *man*.

Although He had done nothing wrong, Jehovah was pleased to crush Him, to strike Him, and to make His whole being (soul) a guilt offering *for mankind*. But Jehovah sees *from where* [Jesus] comes (seed), and that His days are eternal. And the will of Jehovah shall be accomplished in [Jesus'] hand. And [Jesus] will see the labor of His whole being and be satisfied.

"By His knowledge My Righteous Servant shall justify many, for He carried their iniquities. Therefore, I will give Him a portion with the great, and He shall divide the plunder with the strong, because He poured out His whole being unto death and was numbered with the transgressors. And He bore the sins of many and made intercessions for the transgressors.'" (Isaiah 53)

THE LAST WEEK OF
JESUS' MINISTRY
AND THE CROSS

"He was wounded for our transgressions."
(ISAIAH 53:5)

❧ Spring of A.D. 30 ❧

AND THE PASSOVER of the Jews was near, and many went from the country up to Jerusalem. Then they sought Jesus, and spoke among themselves as they stood in the temple, "What do you think—that He will not come to the feast?"

Now both the chief priests and the Pharisees had given a command, that if anyone knew where He was, he should report it, that they might seize Him.

Then six days before the Passover, Jesus came to Bethany, where Lazarus [had been raised from the dead]. Now a great many of the Jews knew that He was there; and they came, not for Jesus' sake only, but that they might also see Lazarus. But the chief priests plotted to put Lazarus to death also, because, [after seeing him], many of the Jews went away and believed in Jesus.

[Jesus and his disciples] drew near Jerusalem, and came to Bethphage, at the Mount of Olives.

Then Jesus sent two disciples, saying to them, "Go into the village opposite you, and immediately you will find a donkey tied, and a colt with her. Loose *them* and bring *them* to Me. And if anyone says anything to you, you shall say, 'The Lord has need of them,' and immediately he will send them."

All this was done that it might be fulfilled which was spoken by the prophet, saying:

> *"Tell the daughter of Zion,*
> *'Behold, your King is coming to you,*
> *Lowly, and sitting on a donkey,*
> *A colt, the foal of a donkey'"*

> (ZECHARIAH 9:9)

THE PRESENTATION OF THE KING

So the disciples went and did as Jesus commanded them. They brought the donkey and the colt, laid their clothes on them, and [Jesus sat] on them.[1] And a very great multitude spread their clothes on the road; others cut down branches from the trees and spread *them* on the road. And the [crowds] who went before and those who followed cried out, saying:

> "Hosanna to the Son of David!
> *'Blessed is He who comes in the name of the*
> LORD!'
> Hosanna in the highest!"[2]

4

Then as Jesus was now drawing near the descent of the Mount of Olives, [a crowd of disciples] began to rejoice and praise God [loudly] for all the mighty works they had seen, saying:

> "*Blessed is the King who comes in the name of the LORD!*"
> Peace in heaven and glory in the highest!"

And some of the Pharisees called to [Jesus] from the crowd, "Teacher, rebuke Your disciples."

[He said to them], "I tell you that if these should keep silent, the stones would immediately cry out."

Now as Jesus drew near, He saw the city and wept over it, saying:

"If [Jerusalem] had known, especially in this your day, the things *that make* for your peace! But now they are hidden from your eyes. For days will come upon you when your enemies will build an embankment around you, surround you, and close you in on every side, and level you, and your children within you, to the ground; and they will not leave in you one stone upon another, because you did not know the time of your visitation."

HEALINGS MAKE THE PRIESTS AND SCRIBES INDIGNANT

And when He had come into Jerusalem, all the city was moved, saying, "Who is this?"

So the [crowds] said, "This is Jesus, the prophet from Nazareth of Galilee."

Then *the* blind and *the* lame came to Him in the temple, and He healed them.

But when the chief priests and scribes saw the wonderful things that He did, and the children crying out in the temple and saying, "Hosanna to the Son of David!" they were indignant and said to [Jesus], "Do You hear what these are saying?"

And Jesus said to them, "Yes. Have you never read,

> *'Out of the mouth of babes and nursing*
>   *infants*
> *You have perfected praise'?"* [3]

Then [Jesus] left them and went out of the city to Bethany, and lodged there.

CURSING A TREE AND CLEANSING THE TEMPLE AGAIN

Now the next day, when they had come out from Bethany, Jesus was hungry. And seeing from afar a fig tree having leaves, He went to see if perhaps He would find something *to eat* on it. When He came to it, He found nothing but leaves, for it was not the season for figs. [4] In response Jesus said to it, "Let no one eat fruit from you ever again." And His disciples heard *it.*

So they came to Jerusalem. [And] Jesus *again* went into the temple and began to drive out those who bought and sold in the temple, and overturned the tables of the money changers and the seats of those who sold doves. And He would not allow anyone to carry wares through the temple. Then He taught, saying to them, "Is it not written, *'My house shall be called a house of prayer for all nations'*? But you have made it a *'den of thieves.'*"[5]

And the scribes and chief priests heard it and sought how they might destroy Him; for they feared Him, because all the people were astonished at His teaching.

DISCUSSION OF JESUS' SUFFERING AND GLORY

Now there were certain Greeks among those who came up to worship at the feast. Then they came to Philip, who was from Bethsaida of Galilee, saying, "Sir, we wish to see Jesus."

Philip came and told Andrew, and in turn Andrew and Philip told Jesus.

But Jesus answered them, saying, "The hour has come that the Son of Man should be glorified. [Truly, truly], I say to you, unless a grain of wheat falls into the ground and dies, it remains alone; but if it dies, it produces much grain.

"He who loves his life will lose it, and he who hates his life in this world will keep it for eternal life. If anyone serves Me, let him follow Me; and where I am, there My servant will be also. If anyone serves Me, him *My* Father will honor.

"Now My soul is troubled, and what shall I say? 'Father, save Me from this hour'? But for this purpose I came to this hour. Father, glorify Your name."

Then a voice came from heaven, *saying,* "I have both glorified *it* and will glorify *it* again."

Therefore the people who stood by and heard *it* said that it had thundered. Others said, "An angel has spoken to Him."

Jesus answered and said, "This voice did not come because of Me, but for your sake. Now is the judgment of this world, and the ruler of this world will be cast out.

"And I, if I am lifted up from the earth, will draw all *peoples* to Myself."

This He said, signifying by what death He would die.

The people answered Him, "We have heard from the law that the Christ remains forever; and how *can* You say, 'The Son of Man must be lifted up'? Who is this Son of Man?"

Then Jesus said to them, "A little while longer the light is with you. Walk while you have the light, [and do not let the] darkness overtake you; he who walks in darkness does not know where he is going. While you have the light, believe in the light, that you may become sons of light."

These things Jesus spoke, and departed, and was hidden from them.

But although He had done so many signs before them, they did not believe in Him, that the word of Isaiah the prophet might be fulfilled, which he spoke:

> "Lord, who has believed our report?
> And to whom has the arm of the
> LORD been revealed?"
>
> (ISAIAH 53:1)

Therefore they could not believe, because Isaiah said again:

> "He has blinded their eyes and
>   hardened their hearts,
> Lest they should see with their eyes,
> Lest they should understand with
>   their hearts and turn,
> So that I should heal them."
>
> (ISAIAH 6:9–10)

These things Isaiah said when he saw His glory and spoke of Him.

SOME BELIEVERS FEAR THE PHARISEES

Nevertheless even among the rulers many believed in Him, but because of the Pharisees they did not confess *Him,* lest they should be put out of the synagogue; for they loved the praise of men more than the praise of God.

Then Jesus cried out and said, "He who believes in Me, believes not in Me but in Him who sent Me. And he who sees Me sees Him who sent Me.

"I have come *as* a light into the world, that whoever believes in Me should not abide in darkness.

"And if anyone hears My words and does not believe, I do not judge him; for I did not come to judge the world but to save the world. He who rejects Me, and does not receive My words, has that which judges him—the word that I have spoken will judge him in the last day.

"For I have not spoken on My own *authority;* but the Father who sent Me gave Me a command, what I should say and what I should speak. And I know that His command is everlasting life. Therefore, whatever I speak, just as the Father has told Me, so I speak."

When evening had come, He went out of the city.

THE BARREN FIG TREE WITHERED

Now in the morning, as [Jesus and His disciples] passed by, they saw the fig tree dried up from the roots.

And Peter, remembering, said to Him, "Rabbi,

look! The fig tree which You cursed has withered away."

So Jesus answered and said to them, "Have faith in God. For [truly], I say to you, whoever says to this mountain, 'Be removed and be cast into the sea,' and does not doubt in his heart, but believes that those things he says will be done, he will have whatever he says. Therefore I say to you, whatever things you ask when you pray, believe that you receive *them*, and you will have *them*.

"And whenever you stand praying, if you have anything against anyone, forgive him, that your Father in heaven may also forgive you your trespasses."

THE RULERS CHALLENGE JESUS

Now when [Jesus] came into the temple, the chief priests and the elders of the people confronted Him as He was teaching, and [they] said, "By what authority are You doing these things? And who gave You this authority?"

But Jesus answered and said to them, "I also will ask you one thing, which if you tell Me, I likewise will tell you by what authority I do these things: The baptism of John—where was it from? From heaven or from men?"

And they reasoned among themselves, saying, "If we say, 'From heaven,' He will say to us, 'Why then did you not believe him?' But if we say, 'From men,' we fear the multitude, for all count John as a prophet." So they answered Jesus and said, "We do not know."

And He said to them, "Neither will I tell you by what authority I do these things.

"But what do you think? A man had two sons, and he came to the first and said, 'Son, go, work today in my vineyard.' He answered and said, 'I will not,' but afterward he regretted it and went.

"Then he came to the second and said likewise. And he answered and said, 'I *go,* sir,' but he did not go. Which of the two did the will of *his* father?"

They said to Him, "The first."

Jesus said to them, "[Truly], I say to you that tax collectors and harlots enter the kingdom of God before you.

For John came to you in the way of righteousness, and you did not believe him; but tax collectors and harlots believed him; and when you saw *it,* you did not afterward relent and believe him.

"Hear another parable:

PARABLE OF THE LANDOWNER— SAME TREATMENT OF JESUS

"There was a certain landowner who planted a vineyard and set a hedge around it, dug a winepress in it and built a tower. And he leased it to vinedressers and went into a far country.

"Now when vintage-time drew near, he sent his servants to the vinedressers, that they might receive its fruit. And the vinedressers took his servants, beat one, killed one, and stoned another.

"Again he sent other servants, more than the first, and they did likewise to them.

"Then last of all he sent his son to them, saying, 'They will respect my son.' But when the vinedressers saw the son, they said among themselves, 'This is the heir. Come, let us kill him and seize his inheritance.'

"So they took him and cast *him* out of the vineyard and killed *him*.

"Therefore, when the owner of the vineyard comes, what will he do to those vinedressers?"

They said to Him, "He will destroy those wicked men miserably, and lease *his* vineyard to other vinedressers who will render to him the fruits in their seasons."

Jesus said to them, "Have you never read in the Scriptures:

> '*The stone which the builders rejected*
> *Has become the chief cornerstone.*
> *This was the LORD's doing,*
> *And it is marvelous in our eyes'?*
> (Psalm 118:22–23)

"Therefore I say to you, the kingdom of God will be taken from you and given to a nation bearing the fruits of it. And whoever falls on this stone will be broken; but on whomever it falls, it will grind him to powder."

Now when the chief priests and Pharisees heard His parables, they perceived that He was speaking of them. But when they sought to lay hands on Him, they feared the crowds, because they took Him for a prophet.

A PARABLE OF A KING

And Jesus answered and spoke to them again by parables and said:

"The kingdom of heaven is like a certain king who arranged a marriage for his son, and sent out his servants to call those who were invited to the wedding; and they were not willing to come.

"Again, he sent out other servants, saying, 'Tell those who are invited, "See, I have prepared my dinner; my oxen and fatted cattle *are* killed, and all things *are* ready. Come to the wedding."' But they made light of it and went their ways, one to his own farm, another to his business. And the rest seized his servants, treated *them* spitefully, and killed *them*.

"But when the king heard *about it,* he was furious. And he sent out his armies, destroyed those murderers, and burned up their city. Then he said to his servants, 'The wedding is ready, but those who were invited were not worthy. *Now,* therefore, go into the highways, and as many as you find, invite to the wedding.'

"So those servants went out into the highways and gathered together all whom they found, both bad and good. And the wedding *hall* was filled with guests.

"But when the king came in to see the guests, he saw a man there who did not have on a wedding garment. So he said to him, 'Friend, how did you come in here without a wedding garment?'

"And he was speechless.

"Then the king said to the servants, 'Bind him hand and foot, take him away, and cast *him* into outer darkness; there will be weeping and gnashing of teeth.'

"For many are called, but few *are* chosen."[6]

PLOTS TO ENTANGLE JESUS

Then the Pharisees went and plotted how they might entangle Him in His talk. And they sent to Him their disciples with the Herodians,[7] saying, "Teacher, we know that You are true, and teach the way of God in truth; nor do You care about anyone, for You do not regard the person of men. Tell us, therefore, what do You think? Is it lawful to pay taxes to Caesar, or not?"

But Jesus perceived their wickedness, and said, "Why do you test Me, *you* hypocrites? Show Me the tax money."

So they brought Him a denarius.

And He said to them, "Whose image and inscription *is* this?"

They said to Him, "Caesar's."

And He said to them, "Render therefore to Caesar the things that are Caesar's, and to God the things that are God's."

When they had heard *these words,* they [were astonished], and left Him and went their way.

THE PLOT OF THE SADDUCEES

The same day the Sadducees, who say there is no resurrection, came to Him and asked Him, saying:

"Teacher, Moses said that if a man dies, having no children, his brother shall marry his wife and raise up offspring for his brother. Now there were with us seven brothers. The first died after he had married, and having no offspring, left his wife to his brother. Likewise the second also, and the third, even to the seventh. Last of all the woman died also. Therefore, in the resurrection, whose wife of the seven will she be? For they all had her."

Jesus answered and said to them, "You are mistaken, not knowing the Scriptures nor the power of God. For in the resurrection they neither marry nor are given in marriage, but are like angels of God in heaven. But concerning the resurrection of the dead, have you not read what was spoken to you by God, saying, *'I am the God of Abraham, the God of Isaac, and the God of Jacob'?*[8]

"God is not the God of the dead, but of the living."

And when the crowds heard *this,* they were astonished at His teaching.

JESUS ANSWERS SOME LEGAL QUESTIONS

Then one of the scribes came, and having heard them reasoning together, perceiving that He had answered them well, asked Him, "Which is the first commandment of all?"

Jesus answered him, "The first of all the commandments *is:* *'Hear, O Israel, the* LORD *our God, the* LORD *is one. And you shall love the* LORD *your God with all your heart, with all your soul, with all your mind, and with all your strength.'* This *is* the first commandment.

"And the second, like *it, is* this: *'You shall love your neighbor as yourself.'*[9]

"There is no other commandment greater than these."

So the scribe said to Him, "Well *said,* Teacher. You have spoken the truth, for there is one God, and there is no other but He. And to love Him with all the heart, with all the understanding, with all the soul, and with all the strength, and to love one's neighbor as oneself, is more than all the whole burnt offerings and sacrifices."

Now when Jesus saw that he answered wisely, He said to him, "You are not far from the kingdom of God."

But after that no one dared question Him.

JESUS DISCUSSES HIS DESCENT FROM DAVID

While the Pharisees were gathered together, Jesus asked them, saying:

"What do you think about the Christ [Messiah]? Whose Son is He?"

They said to Him, "*The Son* of David."

He said to them, "How then does David in the Spirit call Him *'Lord,'* saying:

> *'The LORD said to my Lord,*
> *"Sit at My right hand,*
> *Till I make Your enemies Your footstool"'*?
> (PSALM 110:1)

"If David then calls Him *'Lord,'* how is He his Son?"

And no one was able to answer Him a word, nor from that day on did anyone dare question Him anymore.

JESUS' LAST PUBLIC DISCOURSE

Then Jesus spoke to the [crowds] and to His disciples, saying:

"The scribes and the Pharisees sit in Moses' seat. Therefore whatever they tell you to observe, *that* observe and do, but do not do according to their works; for they say, and do not do.

"For they bind heavy burdens, hard to bear, and lay *them* on men's shoulders; but they *themselves* will not move them with one of their fingers. But all their works they do to be seen by men. They make their phylacteries[10] broad and enlarge the borders of their garments. They love the best places at feasts, the best seats in the synagogues, greetings in the marketplaces, and to be called by men, 'Rabbi, Rabbi.' But you, do not be called 'Rabbi'; for One is your Teacher, the Christ, and you are all brethren.

"Do not call anyone on earth your father; for One is your Father, He who is in heaven.

"And do not be called teachers; for One is your Teacher, the Christ. But he who is greatest among you shall be your servant. And whoever exalts himself will be humbled, and he who humbles himself will be exalted."[11]

A DENUNCIATION OF THE
SCRIBES AND PHARISEES

"But woe to you, scribes and Pharisees, hypocrites! For you shut up the kingdom of heaven against men; for you neither go in *yourselves,* nor do you allow those who are entering to go in.

"Woe to you, scribes and Pharisees, hypocrites! For You devour widows' houses, and for a pretense make long prayers. Therefore you will receive greater condemnation.

"Woe to you, scribes and Pharisees, hypocrites! For you travel land and sea to win one proselyte, and when he is won, you make him twice as much a son of hell as yourselves.

"Woe to you, blind guides, who say, 'Whoever swears by the temple, it is nothing; but whoever swears by the gold of the temple, he is obliged *to perform it.*'

"Fools and blind! For which is greater, the gold or the temple that sanctifies the gold? And, 'Whoever swears by the altar, it is nothing; but whoever swears by the gift that is on it, he is obliged *to perform it.*'

"Fools and blind! For which is greater, the gift or the altar that sanctifies the gift? Therefore he who swears by the altar, swears by it and by all things on it. He who swears by the temple, swears by it and by Him who dwells in it. And he who swears by heaven, swears by the throne of God and by Him who sits on it.

"Woe to you, scribes and Pharisees, hypocrites! For you pay tithe of mint and anise and cummin, and have neglected the weightier *matters* of the law: justice and mercy and faith. These you ought to have done, without leaving the others undone.

"Blind guides, who strain out a gnat and swallow a camel!

"Woe to you, scribes and Pharisees, hypocrites! For you cleanse the outside of the cup and dish, but inside they are full of extortion and self-indulgence.

"Blind Pharisee, first cleanse the inside of the cup and dish, that the outside of them may be clean also.

"Woe to you, scribes and Pharisees, hypocrites! For you are like whitewashed tombs which indeed appear beautiful outwardly, but inside are full of dead *men's* bones and all uncleanness. Even so you also outwardly appear righteous to men, but inside you are full of hypocrisy and lawlessness.

"Woe to you, scribes and Pharisees, hypocrites! Because you build the tombs of the prophets and adorn the monuments of the righteous, and say, 'If we had lived in the days of our fathers, we would not have been partakers with them in the blood of the prophets.'

"Therefore you are witnesses against yourselves that you are sons of those who murdered the prophets."

A FULL MEASURE OF GUILT

"Fill up, then, the measure of your fathers' *guilt*. Serpents, brood of vipers! How can you escape the condemnation of hell?

"Therefore, indeed, I send you prophets, wise men, and scribes: *some* of them you kill and crucify, and *some* of them you scourge in your synagogues and persecute from city to city, that on you may come all the righteous blood shed on the earth, from the blood of righteous Abel to the blood of Zechariah, son of Berechiah, whom you murdered between the temple and the altar. [Truly], I say to you, all these things will come upon this generation."

ANOTHER LAMENT OVER JERUSALEM

"O Jerusalem, Jerusalem, the one who kills the prophets and stones those who are sent to her! How often I wanted to gather your children together, as a hen gathers her chicks under *her* wings, but you were not willing! See! Your house is left to you desolate; for I say to you, you shall see Me no more till you say, *'Blessed is He who comes in the name of the LORD!'*"

(PSALM 118:26).

OBSERVING CONTRIBUTIONS IN THE TEMPLE

Now Jesus sat opposite the treasury and saw how the people put money into the treasury. And many *who were* rich put in much. Then one poor widow came and threw in [two small copper coins].

So [Jesus] called His disciples to *Himself* and said to them, "[Truly], I say to you that this poor widow has put in more than all those who have given to the treasury; for they all put in out of their abundance, but she out of her poverty put in all that she had, her whole livelihood."

IN THE SHADOWS WITH JESUS
A.D. 30

Then Jesus went out and departed from the temple, and His disciples came up to show Him the buildings of the temple. And Jesus said to them, "Do you not see all these things? [Truly], I say to you, not *one* stone shall be left here upon another, that shall not be thrown down."

A SERMON ON THE MOUNT OF OLIVES

Now as He sat on the Mount of Olives, the disciples came to Him privately, saying, "Tell us, when will these things be? And what *will be* the sign of Your coming, and of the end of the age?"

And Jesus answered and said to them: "Take heed that no one deceives you. For many will come in My name, saying, 'I am the Christ,' and will deceive many.

"And you will hear of wars and rumors of wars. See that you are not troubled; for all *these things* must come to pass, but the end is not yet. For nation will rise against nation, and kingdom against kingdom.

"And there will be famines, pestilences, and earthquakes in various places. All these *are* the beginning of sorrows.

"Then they will deliver you up to tribulation and kill you, and you will be hated by all nations for My name's sake. And then many will be offended, will betray one another, and will hate one another."

FALSE PROPHETS TO ARISE

"Then many false prophets will rise up and deceive many. And because lawlessness will abound, the love of many will grow cold.

"But he who endures to the end shall be saved. And this gospel of the kingdom will be preached in all the world as a witness to all the nations, and then the end will come.

"Therefore when you see the *'abomination of desolation,'* spoken of by Daniel the prophet, standing in the holy place" (whoever reads, let him understand), "then let those who are in Judea flee to the mountains. Let him who is on the housetop not go down to take anything out of his house. And let him who is in the field not go back to get his clothes.

"But woe to those who are pregnant and to those who are nursing babies in those days!

"And pray that your flight may not be in winter or on the Sabbath. For then there will be great tribulation, such as has not been since the beginning of the world until this time, no, nor ever shall be. And unless those days were shortened, no flesh would be saved; but for the elect's sake those days will be shortened.

"Then if anyone says to you, 'Look, here *is* the Christ!' or 'There!' do not believe *it*. For false christs and false prophets will rise and show great signs and wonders to deceive, if possible, even the elect. See, I have told you beforehand. Therefore, if they say to you, 'Look, He is in the desert!' do not go out; *or* 'Look, *He is* in the inner rooms!' do not believe *it*. For as the lightning comes from the east and flashes to the west, so also will the coming of the Son of Man be. For wherever the carcass is, there the [vultures] will be gathered together. Immediately after the tribulation of those days the sun will be darkened, and the moon will not give its light; the stars will fall from heaven, and the powers of the heavens will be shaken."

THE SIGN OF THE SECOND COMING OF THE SON OF MAN

"Then the sign of the Son of Man will appear in heaven, and then all the tribes of the earth will mourn, and they will see the Son of Man coming on the clouds of heaven with power and great glory. And He will send His angels with a great sound of a trumpet, and they will gather together His elect from the four winds, from one end of heaven [the firmament] to the other.

"Now learn this parable from the fig tree: When its branch has already become tender and puts forth leaves, you know that summer *is* near. So you also, when you see all these things, know that it is near—at the doors!

"[Truly], I say to you, this generation[12] will by no means pass away till all these things take place. Heaven and earth will pass away, but My words will by no means pass away. But of that day and hour no one knows, not even the angels of heaven, but My Father only."

AS IN THE DAYS OF NOAH

"But as the days of Noah *were,* so also will the coming of the Son of Man be. For as in the days before the flood, they were eating and drinking, marrying and giving in marriage, until the day that Noah entered the ark, and did not know until the flood came and took them all away, so also will the coming of the Son of Man be.

"Then two *men* will be in the field: one will be taken and the other left. Two *women will be* grinding at the mill: one will be taken and the other left.

"Watch therefore, for you do not know what

hour your Lord is coming. But know this, that if the master of the house had known what hour the thief would come, he would have watched and not allowed his house to be broken into.

"Therefore you also be ready, for the Son of Man is coming at an hour you do not expect.

"Who then is a faithful and wise servant, whom his master made ruler over his household, to give them food in due season? Blessed *is* that servant whom his master, when he comes, will find so doing. [Truly], I say to you that he will make him ruler over all his goods.

"But if that evil servant says in his heart, 'My master is delaying his coming,' and begins to beat *his* fellow servants, and to eat and drink with the drunkards, the master of that servant will come on a day when he is not looking for *him* and at an hour that he is not aware of, and will cut him in two and appoint *him* his portion with the hypocrites. There shall be weeping and gnashing of teeth."

THE STORY OF THE TEN VIRGINS

"Then the kingdom of heaven shall be likened to ten virgins who took their lamps and went out to meet the bridegroom. Now five of them were wise, and five *were* foolish. Those who *were* foolish took their lamps and took no oil with them, but the wise took oil in their vessels with their lamps. But while the bridegroom was delayed, they all slumbered and slept.

"And at midnight a cry was *heard:* 'Behold, the bridegroom is coming; go out to meet him!' Then all those virgins arose and trimmed their lamps.

"And the foolish said to the wise, 'Give us *some* of your oil, for our lamps are going out.'

"But the wise answered, saying, '*No,* lest there should not be enough for us and you; but go rather to those who sell, and buy for yourselves.'

"And while they went to buy, the bridegroom came, and those who were ready went in with him to the wedding; and the door was shut. Afterward the other virgins came also, saying, 'Lord, Lord, open to us!' But he answered and said, '[Truly], I say to you, I do not know you.'

"Watch therefore, for you know neither the day nor the hour in which the Son of Man is coming."

LIKE A MAN TRAVELING TO A FAR COUNTRY

"For *the kingdom of heaven is* like a man traveling to a far country, *who* called his own servants and delivered his goods to them.

"And to one he gave five talents, to another two, and to another one, to each according to his own ability; and immediately he went on a journey.

"Then he who had received the five talents went and traded with them, and made another five talents. And likewise he who *had received* two gained two more also. But he who had received one went and dug in the ground, and hid his lord's money.

"After a long time the lord of those servants came and settled accounts with them.

"So he who had received five talents came and brought five other talents, saying, 'Lord, you delivered to me five talents; look, I have gained five more talents besides them.'

"His lord said to him, 'Well *done,* good and faithful servant; you were faithful over a few things, I will make you ruler over many things. Enter into the joy of your lord.'

"He also who had received two talents came and said, 'Lord, you delivered to me two talents; look, I have gained two more talents besides them.'

"His lord said to him, 'Well *done,* good and faithful servant; you have been faithful over a few things, I will make you ruler over many things. Enter into the joy of your lord.'

"Then he who had received the one talent came and said, 'Lord, I knew you to be a hard man, reaping where you have not sown, and gathering where you have not scattered seed. And I was afraid, and went and hid your talent in the ground. Look, *there* you have *what is* yours.'

"But his lord answered and said to him, 'You wicked and lazy servant, you knew that I reap where I have not sown, and gather where I have not scattered seed. So you ought to have deposited my money with the bankers, and at my coming I would have received back my own with interest.

"'So take the talent from him, and give *it* to him who has ten talents. 'For to everyone who has, more will be given, and he will have abundance; but from him who does not have, even what he has will be taken away. And cast the unprofitable servant into the outer darkness. There will be weeping and gnashing of teeth.'

"When the Son of Man comes in His glory, and all the holy angels with Him, then He will sit on the throne of His glory.

"All the nations will be gathered before Him, and He will separate them one from another, as a shepherd divides *his* sheep from the goats."

THE DIVIDING OF THE SHEEP AND GOATS

"And He will set the sheep on His right hand, but the goats on the left.

"Then the King will say to those on His right hand, 'Come, you blessed of My Father, inherit the kingdom prepared for you from the foundation of the world: for I was hungry and you gave Me food; I was thirsty and you gave Me drink; I was a stranger and you took Me in; I *was* naked and you clothed Me; I was sick and you visited Me; I was in prison and you came to Me.'

"Then the righteous will answer Him, saying,

'Lord, when did we see You hungry and feed *You*, or thirsty and give *You* drink? When did we see You a stranger and take *You* in, or naked and clothe *You*? Or when did we see You sick, or in prison, and come to You?' And the King will answer and say to them, '[Truly], I say to you, inasmuch as you did *it* to one of the least of these My brethren, you did *it* to Me.'

"Then He will also say to those on the left hand, 'Depart from Me, you cursed, into the everlasting fire prepared for the devil and his angels: for I was hungry and you gave Me no food; I was thirsty and you gave Me no drink; I was a stranger and you did not take Me in, naked and you did not clothe Me, sick and in prison and you did not visit Me.'

"Then they also will answer Him, saying, 'Lord, when did we see You hungry or thirsty or a stranger or naked or sick or in prison, and did not minister to You?'

"Then He will answer them, saying, '[Truly], I say to you, inasmuch as you did not do *it* to one of the least of these, you did not do *it* to Me.' And these will go away into everlasting punishment, but the righteous into eternal life."

JESUS PREDICTS HIS CRUCIFIXION IN TWO DAYS

Now it came to pass, when Jesus had finished all these sayings, *that* He said to His disciples, "You know that after two days is the Passover, and the Son of Man will be delivered up to be crucified."

THE PLOT TO KILL JESUS

Then the chief priests, the scribes, and the elders of the people assembled at the palace of the high priest, who was called Caiaphas, and plotted to take Jesus by trickery and kill *Him*.

But they said, "Not during the feast, lest there be an uproar among the people."

THE ANOINTING OF JESUS FOR HIS BURIAL

And when Jesus was in Bethany at the house of Simon the leper, there they made Him a supper; and Martha served, but Lazarus was one of those who sat at the table with [Jesus].

Then Mary took a pound of very costly oil of spikenard, anointed the feet of Jesus, and wiped His feet with her hair. And the house was filled with the fragrance of the oil.

But one of His disciples, Judas Iscariot, Simon's *son,* who would betray Him, said, "Why was this fragrant oil not sold for three hundred denarii and given to the poor?" This he said, not that he cared for the poor, but because he was a thief, and had the money box; and he used to take what was put in it. But Jesus said, "Let her alone; she has kept this for the day of My burial. For the poor you have with you always, but Me you do not have always."

"[Truly] I say to you, wherever this gospel is preached in the whole world, what this woman has done will also be told as a memorial to her."

JUDAS BEING REBUKED,
BARGAINS TO BETRAY JESUS

Then Satan entered Judas, surnamed Iscariot, who was numbered among the twelve. So he went his way and conferred with the chief priests and captains, how he might betray [Jesus] to them and said to them, "What are you willing to give me if I deliver Him to you?" And they counted out to him thirty pieces of silver. So from that time he sought opportunity to betray Him.

JESUS PREPARES FOR THE PASSOVER MEAL

Then came the Day of Unleavened Bread, when the Passover must be killed. And [Jesus] sent Peter and John, saying, "Go and prepare the Passover for us, that we may eat." So they said to Him, "Where do You want us to prepare [the meal]?"

And [Jesus] said to them, "Behold, when you have entered the city, a man will meet you carrying a pitcher of water; follow him into the house which he enters. Then you shall say to the master of the house, 'The Teacher [Jesus], says to you, "Where is the guest room where I may eat the Passover with My disciples?"' Then he will show you a large, furnished upper room; there make ready [the Passover meal]."

So they went and found it just as He had said to them, and they prepared the Passover.

When the hour had come, He sat down, and the twelve apostles with Him. Then He said to them, "With *fervent* desire I have desired to eat this Passover with you before I suffer; for I say to you, I will no longer eat of it until it is fulfilled in the kingdom of God."

Now there was also a dispute among them, as to which of them should be considered the greatest. And He said to them, "The kings of the Gentiles exercise lordship over them, and those who exercise authority over them are called 'benefactors.' But not so *among* you; on the contrary, he who is greatest among you, let him be as the younger, and he who governs as he who serves. For who *is* greater, he who sits at the table, or he who serves? *Is* it not he who sits at the table? Yet I am among you as the One who serves.

"But you are those who have continued with Me in My trials. And I bestow upon you a kingdom, just as My Father bestowed *one* upon Me, that you may eat and drink at My table in My kingdom, and sit on thrones judging the twelve tribes of Israel."

JESUS WASHES THE FEET OF HIS DISCIPLES

Now before the Feast of the Passover, when Jesus knew that His hour had come that He should depart from this world to the Father, having loved His own who were in the world, He loved them to the end.

And supper being ended, the devil had already put it into the heart of Judas Iscariot, Simon's *son,* to betray Jesus. Jesus, knowing that the Father had given all things into His hands, that He had come from God, and was going to God, rose from supper and laid aside His garments, took a towel and girded Himself. After that He poured water into a basin and began to wash the disciples' feet, and to wipe *them* with the towel with which He was girded. Then He came to Simon Peter. And *Peter* said to Him, "Lord, are You washing my feet?"

Jesus answered and said to him, "What I am doing you do not understand now, but you will know after this."

Peter said to Him, "You shall never wash my feet!"

Jesus answered him, "If I do not wash you, you have no part with Me."

Simon Peter said to Him, "Lord, not my feet only, but also *my* hands and *my* head!"

Jesus said to him, "He who is bathed needs only to wash *his* feet, but is completely clean; and you are clean, but not all of you." For He knew who would betray Him; therefore He said, "You are not all clean."

So when He had washed their feet, taken His garments, and sat down again, He said to them, "Do you know what I have done to you? You call Me Teacher and Lord, and you say well, for *so* I am. If I then, *your* Lord and Teacher, have washed your feet, you also ought to wash one another's feet. For I have given you an example, that you should do as I have done to you.

"[Most truly], I say to you, a servant is not greater than his master; nor is he who is sent greater than he who sent him. If you know these things, blessed are you if you do them.

"I do not speak concerning all of you. I know whom I have chosen; but that the Scripture may be fulfilled, *'He who eats bread with Me has lifted up his heel against Me.'*[13] Now I tell you before it comes, that when it does come to pass, you may believe that I am *He*.

"[Most truly], I say to you, he who receives whomever I send receives Me; and he who receives Me receives Him who sent Me."

JESUS POINTS OUT JUDAS AS THE BETRAYER

Now as they sat and ate, Jesus said, "[Truly], I say to you, one of you who eats with Me will betray Me."

And they began to be sorrowful, and to say to

Him one by one, "*Is* it I?" And another *said,* "*Is* it I?"

He answered and said to them, "*It is* one of the twelve, who dips with Me in the dish. The Son of Man indeed goes just as it is written of Him, but woe to that man by whom the Son of Man is betrayed! It would have been good for that man if he had never been born."

Now there was leaning on Jesus' bosom one of His disciples, whom Jesus loved. Simon Peter therefore motioned to him to ask who it was of whom He spoke.

Then, leaning back on Jesus' breast, he said to Him, "Lord, who is it?"

Jesus answered, "It is he to whom I shall give a piece of bread when I have dipped *it.*" And having dipped the bread, He gave *it* to Judas Iscariot, *the son* of Simon.

Then Judas, who was betraying Him, answered and said, "Rabbi, is it I?"

He said to him, "You have said it."

Now after the piece of bread, Satan entered him.

Then Jesus said to him, "What you do, do quickly." But no one at the table knew for what reason He said this to him. For some thought, because Judas had the money box, that Jesus had said to him, "Buy *those things* we need for the feast," or that he should give something to the poor.

Having received the piece of bread, he then went out immediately. And it was night.

JESUS WARNS AGAINST DESERTION

So when [Judas] had gone out, Jesus said, "Now the Son of Man is glorified, and God is glorified in Him. [And God will glorify the Son], and glorify Him immediately.

"Little children, I shall be with you a little while longer. You will seek Me; and as I said to the Jews, 'Where I am going, you cannot come.' So now I say to you. A new commandment I give to you, that you love one another; as I have loved you, that you also love one another. By this all will know that you are My disciples, if you have love for one another."

Simon Peter said to Him, "Lord, where are You going?"

Jesus answered him, "Where I am going you cannot follow Me now, but you shall follow Me afterward."

Peter said to Him, "Lord, why can I not follow You now? I will lay down my life for Your sake."

Jesus answered him, "Will you lay down your life for My sake? Most [truly], I say to you, the rooster shall not crow till you have denied Me three times."

And He said to them, "When I sent you without money bag, knapsack, and sandals, did you lack anything?"

So they said, "Nothing."

Then He said to them, "But now, he who has a money bag, let him take *it*, and likewise a knapsack; and he who has no sword, let him sell his garment and buy one. For I say to you that this which is written must still be accomplished in Me: *'And He was numbered with the transgressors.'* For the things concerning Me have an end."

So they said, "Lord, look, here *are* two swords." And He said to them, "It is enough."[14]

JESUS INSTITUTES THE MEMORIAL SUPPER

Then [Jesus] took the cup, and gave thanks, and said, "Take this and divide *it* among yourselves; for I say to you, I will not drink of the fruit of the vine until the kingdom of God comes."

And He took bread, gave thanks and broke *it*, and gave *it* to them, saying, "This is My body which is given for you; do this in remembrance of Me."

Likewise He also *took* the cup after supper, saying, "This cup *is* the new covenant in My blood, which is shed for you. But I say to you, I will not drink of this fruit of the vine from now on until that day when I drink it new with you in My Father's kingdom."

JESUS' FAREWELL DISCOURSE
TO HIS DISCIPLES

"Let not your heart be troubled; you believe in God, believe also in Me. In My Father's house are many mansions; if *it were* not *so,* I would have told you.

"I go to prepare a place for you. And if I go and prepare a place for you, I will come again and receive you to Myself; that where I am, *there* you may be also.

"And where I go you know, and the way you know."

Thomas said to Him, "Lord, we do not know where You are going, and how can we know the way?"

Jesus said to him, "I am the way, the truth, and the life. No one comes to the Father except through Me.

"If you had known Me, you would have known My Father also; and from now on you know Him and have seen Him."

Philip said to Him, "Lord, show us the Father, and it is sufficient for us."

Jesus said to him, "Have I been with you so long, and yet you have not known Me, Philip? He who has seen Me has seen the Father; so how can you say, 'Show us the Father'?

"Do you not believe that I am in the Father, and the Father in Me? The words that I speak to you I do not speak on My own *authority;* but the Father who dwells in Me does the works. Believe Me that I *am* in the Father and the Father in Me, or else believe Me for the sake of the works themselves.

"[Truly, truly], I say to you, he who believes in Me, the works that I do he will do also; and greater *works* than these he will do, because I go to My Father. And whatever you ask in My name, that I will do, that the Father may be glorified in the Son. If you ask anything in My name, I will do *it.*"

A PROMISE OF ANOTHER HELPER

"If you love Me, keep My commandments. And I will pray the Father, and He will give you another Helper, that He may abide with you forever—the Spirit of truth, whom the world cannot receive, because it neither sees Him nor knows Him; but you know Him, for He dwells with you and will be in you. I will not leave you orphans; I will come to you. A little while longer and the world will see Me no more, but you will see Me. Because I live, you will live also. At that day you will know that I *am* in My Father, and you in Me, and I in you. He who has My commandments and keeps them, it is he who loves Me. And he who loves Me will be loved by My Father, and I will love him and manifest Myself to him."

Judas (not Iscariot) said to Him, "Lord, how is it that You will manifest Yourself to us, and not to the world?"

Jesus answered and said to him, "If anyone loves Me, he will keep My word; and My Father will love him, and We will come to him and make Our home with him. He who does not love Me does not keep My words; and the word which you hear is not Mine but the Father's who sent Me.

"These things I have spoken to you while being present with you. But the Helper, the Holy Spirit, whom the Father will send in My name, He will teach you all things, and bring to your remembrance all things that I said to you. Peace I leave with you, My peace I give to you; not as the world gives do I give to you.

"Let not your heart be troubled, neither let it be afraid. You have heard Me say to you, 'I am going away and coming *back* to you.' If you loved Me, you would rejoice because I said, 'I am going to the Father,' for My Father is greater than I. And now I have told you before it comes, that when it does come to pass, you may believe. I will no longer talk much with you, for the ruler of this world is coming, and he has nothing in Me. But that the world may know that I love the Father, and as the Father gave Me commandment, so I do. Arise, let us go from here."

THE DISCOURSE ON THE
WAY TO GETHSEMANE

"I am the true vine, and My Father is the vine-dresser. Every branch in Me that does not bear fruit He [lifts up]; and every *branch* that bears fruit He prunes, that it may bear more fruit. You are already clean because of the word which I have spoken to you. Abide in Me, and I in you. As the branch cannot bear fruit of itself, unless it abides in the vine, neither can you, unless you abide in Me.

"I am the vine, you *are* the branches. He who abides in Me, and I in him, bears much fruit; for without Me you can do nothing. If anyone does not abide in Me, he is cast out as a branch and is withered; and they gather them and throw *them* into the fire, and they are burned.

"If you abide in Me, and My words abide in you, you will ask what you desire, and it shall be done for you. By this My Father is glorified, that you bear much fruit; so you will be My disciples.

"As the Father loved Me, I also have loved you; abide in My love. If you keep My commandments, you will abide in My love, just as I have kept My Father's commandments and abide in His love. These things I have spoken to you, that My joy may remain in you, and *that* your joy may be full. This is My commandment, that you love one another as I have loved you. Greater love has no one than this, than to lay down one's life for his friends. You are My friends if you do whatever I command you. No longer do I call you servants, for a servant does not know what his master is doing; but I have called you friends, for all things that I heard from My Father I have made known to you. You did not choose Me, but I chose you and appointed you that you should go and bear fruit, and *that* your fruit should remain, that whatever you ask the Father in My name He may give you. These things I command you, that you love one another.

"If the world hates you, you know that it hated Me before *it hated* you. If you were of the world, the world would love its own. Yet because you are not of the world, but I chose you out of the world, therefore the world hates you.

"Remember the word that I said to you, 'A servant is not greater than his master.' If they persecuted Me, they will also persecute you. If they kept My word, they will keep yours also.

"But all these things they will do to you for My name's sake, because they do not know Him who sent Me. If I had not come and spoken to them, they would have no sin, but now they have no excuse for their sin. He who hates Me hates My Father also.

"If I had not done among them the works which no one else did, they would have no sin; but now they have seen and also hated both Me and My Father. But *this happened* that the word might be fulfilled which is written in their law, '*They hated Me without a cause*.'[15]

"But when the Helper comes, whom I shall send to you from the Father, the Spirit of truth who proceeds from the Father, He will testify of

Me. And you also will bear witness, because you have been with Me from the beginning.

"These things I have spoken to you, that you should not be made to stumble. They will put you out of the synagogues; yes, the time is coming that whoever kills you will think that he offers God service. And these things they will do to you because they have not known the Father nor Me.

"But these things I have told you, that when the time comes, you may remember that I told you of them.

"And these things I did not say to you at the beginning, because I was with you."

OTHER PROMISES ABOUT
OUR HEAVENLY HELPER

"But now I go away to Him who sent Me, and none of you asks Me, 'Where are You going?' But because I have said these things to you, sorrow has filled your heart. Nevertheless I tell you the truth. It is to your advantage that I go away; for if I do not go away, the Helper will not come to you; but if I depart, I will send Him to you.

"And when He has come, He will convict the world of sin, and of righteousness, and of judgment: of sin, because they do not believe in Me; of righteousness, because I go to My Father and you see Me no more; of judgment, because the ruler of this world is judged.

"I still have many things to say to you, but you cannot bear *them* now. However, when He, the Spirit of truth, has come, He will guide you into all truth; for He will not speak on His own *authority,* but whatever He hears He will speak; and He will tell you things to come. He will glorify Me, for He will take of what is Mine and declare *it* to you. All things that the Father has are Mine. Therefore I said that He will take of Mine and declare *it* to you.

"A little while, and you will not see Me; and again a little while, and you will see Me, because I go to the Father."

Then *some* of His disciples said among themselves, "What is this that He says to us, 'A little while, and you will not see Me; and again a little while, and you will see Me'; and, 'because I go to the Father'?" They said therefore, "What is this that He says, 'A little while'? We do not know what He is saying."

Now Jesus knew that they desired to ask Him, and He said to them, "Are you inquiring among yourselves about what I said, 'A little while, and you will not see Me; and again a little while, and you will see Me'? [Truly, truly], I say to you that you will weep and lament, but the world will rejoice; and you will be sorrowful, but your sorrow will be turned into joy.

"A woman, when she is in labor, has sorrow because her hour has come; but as soon as she has given birth to the child, she no longer remembers the anguish, for joy that a human being has been born into the world."

SORROW WILL TURN TO JOY

"Therefore you now have sorrow; but I will see you again and your heart will rejoice, and your joy no one will take from you.

"And in that day you will ask Me nothing. [Truly, truly], I say to you, whatever you ask the Father in My name He will give you. Until now you have asked nothing in My name. Ask, and you will receive, that your joy may be full.

"These things I have spoken to you in figurative language; but the time is coming when I will no longer speak to you in figurative language, but I will tell you plainly about the Father. In that day you will ask in My name, and I do not say to you that I shall pray the Father for you; for the Father Himself loves you, because you have loved Me, and have believed that I came forth from God. I came forth from the Father and have come into the world. Again, I leave the world and go to the Father."

His disciples said, "See, now You are speaking plainly, and using no figure of speech! Now we are sure that You know all things, and have no need that anyone should question You. By this we believe that You came forth from God."

Jesus answered them, "Do you now believe? Indeed the hour is coming, yes, has now come, that you will be scattered, each to his own, and will leave Me alone. And yet I am not alone, because the Father is with Me. These things I have spoken to you, that in Me you may have peace. In the world you will have tribulation; but be of good cheer, I have overcome the world."

CHRIST'S GREAT INTERCESSORY PRAYER

Jesus spoke these words, lifted up His eyes to heaven, and said:

"Father, the hour has come. Glorify Your Son, that Your Son also may glorify You, as You have given Him authority over all flesh, that He should give eternal life to as many as You have given Him. And this is eternal life, that they may know You, the only true God, and Jesus Christ whom You have sent.

"I have glorified You on the earth. I have finished the work which You have given Me to do. And now, O Father, glorify Me together with Yourself, with the glory which I had with You before the world was.

"I have manifested Your name to the men whom You have given Me out of the world. They were Yours, You gave them to Me, and they have kept Your word. Now they have known that all things which You have given Me are from You. For

I have given to them the words which You have given Me; and they have received *them,* and have known surely that I came forth from You; and they have believed that You sent Me.

"I pray for them. I do not pray for the world but for those whom You have given Me, for they are Yours. And all Mine are Yours, and Yours are Mine, and I am glorified in them.

"Now I am no longer in the world, but these are in the world, and I come to You. Holy Father, keep through Your name those whom You have given Me, that they may be one as We *are.* While I was with them in the world, I kept them in Your name. Those whom You gave Me I have kept; and none of them is lost except the son of perdition, that the Scripture might be fulfilled.

"But now I come to You, and these things I speak in the world, that they may have My joy fulfilled in themselves. I have given them Your word; and the world has hated them because they are not of the world, just as I am not of the world. I do not pray that You should take them out of the world, but that You should keep them from the evil one. They are not of the world, just as I am not of the world. Sanctify them by Your truth. Your word is truth.

"As You sent Me into the world, I also have sent them into the world. And for their sakes I sanctify Myself, that they also may be sanctified by the truth.

"I do not pray for these alone, but also for those who will believe in Me through their word; that they all may be one, as You, Father, *are* in Me, and I in You; that they also may be one in Us, that the world may believe that You sent Me. And the glory which You gave Me I have given them, that they may be one just as We are one: I in them, and You in Me; that they may be made perfect in one, and that the world may know that You have sent Me, and have loved them as You have loved Me. Father, I desire that they also whom You gave Me may be with Me where I am, that they may behold My glory which You have given Me; for You loved Me before the foundation of the world.

"O righteous Father! The world has not known You, but I have known You; and these have known that You sent Me. I have declared to them Your name, and will declare *it,* that the love with which You loved Me may be in them, and I in them."

JESUS' AGONY IN GETHSEMANE

When Jesus had spoken these words, they sang a hymn, and He went out with His disciples over the Brook Kidron, where there was a garden called Gethsemane. [He] said to the disciples, "Sit here while I go and pray over there."

And He took with Him Peter and the two sons of Zebedee, and He began to be sorrowful and deeply distressed.

Then He said to them, "My soul is exceedingly sorrowful, even to death. Stay here and watch with Me."

He went a little farther and fell on His face, and prayed, saying, "O My Father, if it is possible, let this cup pass from Me; nevertheless, not as I will, but as You *will*."

Then He came to the disciples and found them sleeping, and [He] said to Peter, "What! Could you not watch with Me one hour? Watch and pray, lest you enter into temptation. The spirit indeed *is* willing, but the flesh *is* weak."

Again, a second time, He went away and prayed saying, "O My Father, if this cup cannot pass away from Me unless I drink it, Your will be done." And He came and found them asleep again, for their eyes were heavy. So He left them, went away again, and prayed the third time, saying the same words.

Then He came to His disciples and said to them, "Are *you* still sleeping and resting? Behold, the hour is at hand, and the Son of Man is being betrayed into the hands of sinners. Rise, let us be going. See, My betrayer is at hand."

BETRAYED, ARRESTED AND FORSAKEN

And Judas, who betrayed [Jesus], also knew the place; for Jesus often met there with His disciples. Then Judas, having received a detachment *of troops,* and officers from the chief priests and Pharisees, came there with lanterns, torches, and weapons. Jesus therefore, knowing all things that would come upon Him, went forward and said to them, "Whom are you seeking?"

They answered Him, "Jesus of Nazareth."

Jesus said to them, "I am *He.*"

And Judas, who betrayed Him, also stood with them.

Now when Jesus said to them, "I am *He,*" they drew back and fell to the ground.

Then He asked them again, "Whom are you seeking?"

And they said, "Jesus of Nazareth."

Jesus answered, "I have told you that I am *He.* Therefore, if you seek Me, let these go their way," that the saying might be fulfilled which He spoke, "Of those whom You gave Me I have lost none."

THE KISS OF DEATH

Now His betrayer had given them a sign, saying, "Whomever I kiss, He is the One; seize Him."

Immediately, [Judas] went up to Jesus and said, "Greetings, Rabbi!" and kissed Him.

But Jesus said to him, "Friend, why have you come?"

Then they came and laid hands on Jesus and took Him.

Then Simon Peter, having a sword, drew it and

struck the high priest's servant, and cut off his right ear. The servant's name was Malchus.

So Jesus said to Peter, "Put your sword into the sheath. Shall I not drink the cup which My Father has given Me? Or do you think that I cannot now pray to My Father, and He will provide Me with more than twelve legions of angels? How then could the Scriptures be fulfilled, that it must happen thus?"

In that hour, Jesus said to the [crowds], "Have you come out as against a robber, with swords and clubs to take Me? I sat daily with you, teaching in the temple, and you did not seize Me."

Then all the disciples forsook Him and fled.

Now a certain young man followed Him, having a linen cloth thrown around *his* naked *body.* And the young men laid hold of him, and he left the linen cloth and fled from them naked.[16]

JESUS FIRST EXAMINED BY ANNAS, THE EX-HIGH PRIEST

Then the detachment *of troops* and the captain and the officers of the Jews arrested Jesus and bound Him. And they led Him away to Annas first, for he was the father-in-law of Caiaphas who was high priest that year. Now it was Caiaphas who advised the Jews that it was expedient that one man should die for the people.

The high priest then asked Jesus about His disciples and His doctrine.

Jesus answered him, "I spoke openly to the world. I always taught in synagogues and in the temple, where the Jews always meet, and in secret I have said nothing. Why do you ask Me? Ask those who have heard Me what I said to them. Indeed they know what I said."

And when He had said these things, one of the officers who stood by struck Jesus with the palm of his hand, saying, "Do You answer the high priest like that?"

Jesus answered him, "If I have spoken evil, bear witness of the evil; but if well, why do you strike Me?"

JESUS HURRIEDLY TRIED AND CONDEMNED

And those who had laid hold of Jesus led *Him* away to Caiaphas the high priest, where the scribes and the elders were assembled. Now the chief priests, the elders, and all the council sought false testimony against Jesus to put Him to death, but found none.

Even though many false witnesses came forward, they found none. But at last two false witnesses came forward and said, "This *fellow* said, 'I am able to destroy the temple of God and to build it in three days.'"

And the high priest arose and said to Him, "Do

You answer nothing? What *is it* these men testify against You?"

But Jesus kept silent. And the high priest answered and said to Him, "I put You under oath by the living God: Tell us if You are the Christ, the Son of God!"

Jesus said to him, "*It is as* you said. Nevertheless, I say to you, hereafter you will see the Son of Man sitting at the right hand of the Power, and coming on the clouds of heaven."

Then the high priest tore his clothes, saying, "He has spoken blasphemy! What further need do we have of witnesses? Look, now you have heard His blasphemy! What do you think?"

They answered and said, "He is deserving of death." Then they spat in His face and beat Him; and others struck *Him* with the palms of their hands, saying, "Prophesy to us, Christ! Who is the one who struck You?"

PETER DENIES HIS LORD THREE TIMES

And Simon Peter followed Jesus, and so *did* another disciple. Now that disciple was known to the high priest, and went with Jesus into the courtyard of the high priest. But Peter stood at the door outside. Then the other disciple, who was known to the high priest, went out and spoke to her who kept the door, and brought Peter in. Then the servant girl who kept the door said to Peter, "You are not also *one* of this Man's disciples, are you?"

Peter said, "I am not."

Now the servants and officers who had made a fire of coals stood there, for it was cold, and they warmed themselves. And Peter stood with them and warmed himself.

And when he had gone out to the gateway, another *girl* saw him and said to those *who were* there, "This *fellow* also was with Jesus of Nazareth."

But again [Peter] denied with an oath, "I do not know the Man!"

And a little later those who stood by came up and said to Peter, "Surely you also are *one* of them, for your speech betrays you."

Then he began to curse and swear, *saying,* "I do not know the Man!" Immediately a rooster crowed. And Peter remembered the word of Jesus who had said to him, "Before the rooster crows, you will deny Me three times."

So [Peter] went out and wept bitterly.

The Gospel accounts of Peters' denial vary in details. Matthew tells of a "servant girl" and "another girl." And Mark tells of a "servant girl" who twice confronted Peter. The accounts of denial to the "servant girls" and others are three in number as Jesus had said. The reading here was a blending of the Gospel accounts.

JESUS IS FORMALLY CONDEMNED BY THE SANHEDRIN[17]

As soon as it was day, the elders of the people, both chief priests and scribes, came together and led [Jesus] into their council, saying, "If You are the Christ, tell us."

But [Jesus] said to them, "If I tell you, you will by no means believe. And if I also ask *you*, you will by no means answer Me or let *Me* go. Hereafter the Son of Man will sit on the right hand of the power of God."

Then they all said, "Are You then the Son of God?"

So He said to them, "You *rightly* say that I am."

And they said, "What further testimony do we need? For we have heard it ourselves from His own mouth."

REMORSE AND SUICIDE OF JUDAS

Then Judas, His betrayer, seeing that [Jesus] had been condemned, was remorseful and brought back the thirty pieces of silver to the chief priests and elders, saying, "I have sinned by betraying innocent blood."

And they said, "What *is that* to us? You see *to it!*"

Then he threw down the pieces of silver in the temple and departed, and went and hanged himself.

But the chief priests took the silver pieces and said, "It is not lawful to put them into the treasury, because they are the price of blood." And they consulted together and bought with [the pieces of silver] the potter's field to bury strangers in. Therefore that field has been called the Field of Blood to this day. Then was fulfilled what was spoken by Jeremiah the prophet, saying, *"And they took the thirty pieces of silver, the value of Him who was priced,* whom they of the children of Israel priced, *and gave them for the potter's field, as the* LORD *directed me."*[18]

JESUS' FIRST TIME BEFORE PILATE, GOVERNOR OF JUDEA

Then they led Jesus from Caiaphas to the Praetorium, and it was early morning. But they themselves did not go into the Praetorium, lest they should be defiled [and not able to eat the Passover]. Pilate then went out to them and said, "What accusation do you bring against this Man?"

They answered and said to him, "If He were not an evildoer, we would not have delivered Him up to you."

And they began to accuse Him, saying, "We found this *fellow* perverting the nation, and forbidding to pay taxes to Caesar, saying that He Himself is Christ, a King."

Then Pilate said to them, "You take Him and judge Him according to your law."

Therefore the Jews said to him, "It is not lawful for us to put anyone to death." [The words of Jesus being fulfilled, signifying by what death He would die].

Then Pilate entered the Praetorium again, called Jesus, and said to Him, "Are You the King of the Jews?"

Jesus answered him, "Are you speaking for yourself about this, or did others tell you this concerning Me?"

Pilate answered, "Am I a Jew? Your own nation and the chief priests have delivered You to me. What have You done?"

Jesus answered, "My kingdom is not of this world. If My kingdom were of this world, My servants would fight, so that I should not be delivered to the Jews; but now My kingdom is not from here."

Pilate therefore said to Him, "Are You a king then?"

Jesus answered, "You say *rightly* that I am a king. For this cause I was born, and for this cause I have come into the world, that I should bear witness to the truth. Everyone who is of the truth hears My voice."

Pilate said to Him, "What is truth?"

And when he had said this, he went out again to the Jews, and said to them, "I find no fault in Him at all."

And while [Jesus] was being accused by the chief priests and elders, He answered nothing.

Then Pilate said to [Jesus], "Do You not hear how many things they testify against You?" But [Jesus] answered him not one word, so that the governor [was greatly amazed].

But they were the more fierce, saying, "He stirs up the people, teaching throughout all Judea, beginning from Galilee to this place."

JESUS BEFORE HEROD, GOVERNOR OF GALILEE

When Pilate heard of Galilee, he asked if the Man were a Galilean. And as soon as he knew that He belonged to Herod's jurisdiction, he sent Him to Herod, who was also in Jerusalem at that time.

Now when Herod saw Jesus, he was exceedingly glad; for he had desired for a long *time* to see Him, because he had heard many things about Him, and he hoped to see some miracle done by Him. Then he questioned [Jesus] with many words, but [Jesus] answered him nothing. And the chief priests and scribes stood and vehemently accused Him. Then Herod, with his men of war, treated Him with contempt and mocked

Him, arrayed Him in a gorgeous robe, and sent Him back to Pilate.

That very day Pilate and Herod became friends with each other, for previously they had been at enmity with each other.

JESUS BEFORE PILATE THE SECOND TIME

Now at the feast [Pilate] was accustomed to releasing one prisoner to them, whomever they requested. And there was one named Barabbas, *who was* chained with his fellow rebels; they had committed murder in the rebellion.

Then the multitude, crying aloud, began to ask *him to do* just as he had always done for them.

Then Pilate, when he had called the chief priests, the rulers, and the people, said to them, "You have brought this Man to me, as one who misleads the people. And indeed, having examined *Him* in your presence, I have found no fault in this Man concerning those things of which you accuse Him; no, neither did Herod, for I sent You back to him; and indeed nothing deserving of death has been done by Him."

Therefore, when they had gathered together, Pilate said to them, "Whom do you want me to release to you? Barabbas, or Jesus who is called Christ?" For he knew that they had handed Him over because of envy.

A MESSAGE FROM PILATE'S WIFE IS IGNORED

While [Pilate] was sitting on the judgment seat, his wife sent to him, saying, "Have nothing to do with that just Man, for I have suffered many things today in a dream because of Him."

But the chief priests and elders persuaded the multitudes that they should ask for Barabbas and destroy Jesus.

The governor answered and said to them, "Which of the two do you want me to release to you?"

They said, "Barabbas!"

And they all cried out at once, saying, "Away with this *Man,* and release to us Barabbas"—who had been thrown into prison for a certain rebellion made in the city, and for murder.

PILATE'S CONTINUED DELAY

So then Pilate took Jesus and scourged *Him.*[19] Then the soldiers of the governor took Jesus into the Praetorium, [gathering] the whole garrison around Him.

And the soldiers twisted a crown of thorns and put *it* on His head. [They stripped Him], and they put on Him a purple robe. [Then] they bowed the knee before Him, and mocked Him, saying, "Hail, King of the Jews!" [And] they spat on Him and slapped Him with their hands. Then, they took [a] reed and struck Him on the head.

Pilate then went out again, and said to them, "Behold, I am bringing Him out to you that you may know that I find no fault in Him."

Then Jesus came out, wearing the crown of thorns and the purple robe. And *Pilate* said to them, "Behold the Man!"

The present reading is a blending of passages from the four Gospels. For an understanding of the robes Jesus wore during His passion, see the discussion, **The Robes Jesus Wore on page 109.**

Therefore when the chief priests and officers saw Him, they cried out, saying, "Crucify *Him,* crucify *Him!*"

Pilate said to them, "You take Him and crucify *Him,* for I find no fault in Him."

The Jews answered him, "We have a law, and according to our law He ought to die, because He made Himself the Son of God."

Therefore, when Pilate heard that saying, he was the more afraid, and went again into the Praetorium, and said to Jesus, "Where are You from?" But Jesus gave him no answer.

Then Pilate said to Him, "Are You not speaking

to me? Do You not know that I have power to crucify You, and power to release You?"

Jesus answered, "You could have no power at all against Me unless it had been given you from above. Therefore, the one who delivered Me to you has the greater sin."

[Pilate continued to try and release Jesus]. But the Jews cried out, saying, "If you let this Man go, you are not Caesar's friend. Whoever makes himself a king speaks against Caesar."

When Pilate therefore heard that saying, he brought Jesus out and sat down in the judgment seat in a place that is called *The* Pavement, but in Hebrew, Gabbatha.

Now it was the Preparation Day of the Passover, and about the sixth hour, and [Pilate] said to the Jews, "Behold your King!"

But they cried out, "Away with *Him,* away with *Him!* Crucify Him!"

Pilate said to them, "Shall I crucify your King?"

The chief priests answered, "We have no king but Caesar!"

PILATE COULD NOT PREVAIL

When Pilate saw that he could not prevail at all, but rather *that* a tumult was rising, he took water and washed *his* hands before the [crowd], saying, "I am innocent of the blood of this just Person. You see *to it*."

And all the people answered and said, "His blood *be* on us and on our children."

Then [Pilate] released Barabbas to them, [and he delivered Jesus to be crucified.]

And when they had mocked Him, they took the purple robe off Him, put His own clothes on Him, and led Him out to crucify Him.

Then they compelled a certain man, Simon a Cyrenian, the father of Alexander and Rufus, as he was coming out of the country and passing by, to bear His cross.

And a great [crowd] of the people followed Him, and women who also mourned and lamented Him.

But Jesus, turning to them, said, "Daughters of Jerusalem, do not weep for Me, but weep for yourselves and for your children. For indeed the days are coming in which they will say, 'Blessed *are* the barren, wombs that never bore, and breasts which never nursed!' Then they will begin *'to say to the mountains, "Fall on us!" and to the hills, "Cover us!"'* [If these are done when the tree is green, what shall happen when it is dry?"]

There were also two others, criminals, led with Him to be put to death. And when they had come to a place called Golgotha, that is to say, Place of a Skull, they gave Him sour wine [mixed] with gall to drink. But when He had tasted *it,* He would not drink.

THE FIRST THREE HOURS ON THE CROSS

There they crucified Him, and the criminals, one on the right hand and the other on the left. Then Jesus said, "Father, forgive them, for they do not know what they do."

Then the soldiers, when they had crucified Jesus, took His garments and made four parts, to each soldier a part, and also the tunic. Now the tunic was without seam, woven from the top in one piece.

They said therefore among themselves, "Let us not tear it, but cast lots for it, whose it shall be," that the Scripture might be fulfilled which says:

"They divided My garments among them,
And for My clothing they cast lots."
(PSALM 22:18)

Now Pilate wrote a title and put *it* on the cross. And the writing was:

JESUS OF NAZARETH, THE KING OF THE JEWS

Then many of the Jews read this title, for the place where Jesus was crucified was near the city; and it was written in Hebrew, Greek, *and* Latin.

Therefore the chief priests of the Jews said to Pilate, "Do not write, 'The King of the Jews,' but, 'He said, "I am the King of the Jews.""'

Pilate answered, "What I have written, I have written."

The following is a blending of the accounts from the Gospels. See the List of Scriptures for these accounts at the end of this work.

And those who passed by blasphemed [Jesus], wagging their heads and saying, "You who destroy the temple and build *it* in three days, save Yourself! If You are the Son of God, come down from the cross." Likewise, the chief priests also, mocking with the scribes and elders, said, "He saved others; Himself He cannot save. If He is the King of Israel, let Him now come down from the cross, and we will believe Him. He trusted in God; let Him deliver Him now if He will have Him; for He said, 'I am the Son of God.'"

Even the robbers who were crucified with [Jesus] reviled Him with the same thing. Then one of the criminals who were hanged blasphemed Him, saying, "If You are the Christ, save Yourself and us."

But the other, answering, rebuked him, saying, "Do you not even fear God, seeing you are under the same condemnation? [We deserve this. We receive what is due for our deeds], but this Man has done nothing wrong." Then he said to Jesus,

"Lord, remember me when You come into Your kingdom."

And Jesus said to him, "[Truly], I say to you, today you will be with Me in Paradise."

Now there stood by the cross of Jesus His mother, and His mother's sister, Mary the *wife* of Clopas, and Mary Magdalene. When Jesus therefore saw His mother, and the disciple whom He loved standing by [her], He said, "Woman, behold your son!" Then He said to the disciple, "Behold your mother!" And from that hour that disciple took her to his own *home.*

THE THREE HOURS OF DARKNESS (12 NOON TO 3 P.M.)

Now from the sixth hour until the ninth hour there was darkness over all the land. And about the ninth hour Jesus cried out with a loud voice, saying, "Eli, Eli, lama sabachthani?" that is, *"My God, My God, why have You forsaken Me?"* (Psalm 22:1.)

Some of those who stood there, when they heard [this], said, "This Man is calling for Elijah!"

After this, Jesus, knowing that all things were now accomplished, that the Scripture might be fulfilled, said, "I thirst!"

Now a vessel full of sour wine was sitting there; and immediately one of them ran and took a sponge, filled it with sour wine and put it on a reed, and put *it* to His mouth.

So when Jesus had received the sour wine, He said, "It is finished!" He cried out with a loud voice, saying, "Father, into Your hands I commit My spirit." Then, breathing His last breath, He bowed His head and gave up His spirit.

THE PHENOMENA
ACCOMPANYING CHRIST'S DEATH

Then, behold, the veil of the temple was torn in two from top to bottom; and the earth quaked, and the rocks were split, and the graves were opened; and many bodies of the saints who had fallen asleep were raised; and coming out of the graves after His resurrection, they went into the holy city and appeared to many.

So when the centurion and those with him, who were guarding Jesus, saw the earthquake and the things that had happened, they feared greatly, saying, "Truly this was the Son of God!"

And many women who followed Jesus from Galilee, ministering to Him, were there looking on from afar, among whom were Mary Magdalene, Mary the mother of James and Joses, and the mother of Zebedee's sons.

THE BURIAL OF THE BODY OF JESUS

Therefore, because it was the Preparation *Day*, that the bodies should not remain on the cross on the Sabbath (for that Sabbath was a high day), the Jews asked Pilate that their legs might be broken, and *that* they might be taken away.

Then the soldiers came and broke the legs of the first and of the other who was crucified with [Jesus]. But when they came to Jesus and saw that He was already dead, they did not break His legs.

But one of the soldiers pierced His side with a spear, and immediately blood and water came out. And he who has seen has testified, and his testimony is true; and he knows that he is telling the truth, so that you may believe. For these things were done that the Scripture should be fulfilled, *"Not one of His bones shall be broken."*[20] And again another Scripture says, *"They shall look on Him whom they pierced."*[21]

After this, Joseph of Arimathea, being a disciple of Jesus, but secretly, for fear of the Jews, asked Pilate that he might take away the body of Jesus; and Pilate gave *him* permission.

So Joseph came and took the body of Jesus.

And Nicodemus, who at first came to Jesus by night, also came, bringing a mixture of myrrh and aloes, about a hundred pounds. Then they took the body of Jesus, and bound it in strips of linen with the spices, as the custom of the Jews is to bury.

Now in the place where He was crucified there was a garden, and in the garden a new tomb in which no one had yet been laid. So there they laid

Jesus, because of the Jews' Preparation *Day*, for the tomb was nearby.

THE WATCH OF THE WOMEN
AT THE TOMB OF JESUS

And the women who had come with Him from Galilee followed after, and they observed the tomb and how His body was laid. Then they returned and prepared spices and fragrant oils. And they rested on the Sabbath according to the commandment.

On the next day, which followed the Day of Preparation, the chief priests and Pharisees gathered together to Pilate, saying, "Sir, we remember, while He was still alive, how that deceiver said, 'After three days I will rise.' Therefore command that the tomb be made secure until the third day, lest His disciples come by night and steal Him *away*, and say to the people, 'He has risen from the dead.' So the last deception will be worse than the first."

Pilate said to them, "You have a guard; go your way, make *it* as secure as you know how." So they went and made the tomb secure, sealing the stone and setting the guard.

RESURRECTION AND ASCENSION OF JESUS CHRIST

"Christ the Lord is risen today, Alleluia!"
(CHARLES WESLEY)

∽ Spring A.D. 30 ∽

AND BEHOLD, there was a great earthquake! For an angel of the Lord descended from heaven, and came and rolled back the stone from the door, and sat on it. His countenance was as lightning, and his clothing as white as snow. And the guards shook [with] fear of him, and [they] became like dead men.

The exact order of every single event in the first few hours after the resurrection of Jesus is difficult to positively establish chronologically, though a general order is understood. From the beginning of this section and throughout, some blending of the Gospel accounts relating to the resurrection of Jesus is used in what seems to be a logical order. Someone else may give a somewhat different order.

THE FIRST DAY OF THE WEEK

Now *it was* the first day of the week, and it was still dark.[1] And Mary Magdalene, Mary *the mother* of James, and Salome, *with* certain *other women*, came to the tomb with spices which they had prepared, that they could anoint *the body of* Jesus.

But they found the stone rolled away from the tomb.

Then they went in and did not find the body of the Lord Jesus.

And it happened, as they were greatly perplexed about this, that behold, two men stood by them in shining garments. Then as they were afraid and bowed *their* faces to the earth, [the men] said to them, "Why do you seek the living among the dead? He is not here, but is risen! Remember how He spoke to you when He was still in Galilee, saying, 'The Son of Man must be delivered into the hands of sinful men, and be crucified, and the third day rise again.'"

And they remembered [Jesus'] words.

Then they returned from the tomb and told all these things to the eleven and to all the rest, and their words seemed like idle tales, and they did not believe them.

Peter therefore went out, and the other disciple [John], and were going to the tomb. So they both ran together, and the other disciple outran Peter and came to the tomb first. And he, stooping down and looking in, saw the linen cloths lying *there;* yet he did not go in.

Then Simon Peter came, following him, and went into the tomb; and he saw the linen cloths lying *there,* and the handkerchief that had been around His head, not lying with the linen cloths, but folded together in a place by itself. Then the other disciple, who came to the tomb first, went in also; and he saw and believed.

THE FIRST APPEARANCE
OF THE RISEN LORD

Mary Magdalene, who, with the other women, had reported these things to Peter, had returned and was standing outside the tomb after Peter had departed. She was the first to whom Jesus appeared.

But Mary stood outside by the tomb weeping, and as she wept she stooped down *and looked* into the tomb. And she saw two angels in white sitting, one at the head and the other at the feet, where the body of Jesus had lain. Then they said to her, "Woman, why are you weeping?"

She said to them, "Because they have taken away my Lord, and I do not know where they have laid Him."

Now when she had said this, she turned around and saw Jesus standing *there,* and did not know that it was Jesus.

Jesus said to her, "Woman, why are you weeping? Whom are you seeking?"

She, supposing Him to be the gardener, said to Him, "Sir, if You have carried Him away, tell me where You have laid Him, and I will take Him away."

Jesus said to her, "Mary!"

She turned and said to Him, "Rabboni!" (which is to say, Teacher).

Jesus said to her, "Do not cling to Me, for I have not yet ascended to My Father; but go to My brethren and say to them, 'I am ascending to My Father and your Father, and *to* My God and your God.'"

Mary Magdalene came and told the disciples that she had seen the Lord, and *that* He had spoken these things to her.

[The other women were on their way to tell the disciples these things, and behold, Jesus met them, saying, "Rejoice!" And they came and held Him by the feet and worshiped Him.]

Then Jesus said to them, "Do not be afraid. Go *and* tell My brothers to go to Galilee, and there they will see Me."

THE GUARD'S REPORT
TO THE JEWISH RULERS

Now while [the women] were going, behold, some of the guard came into the city and reported to the chief priests all the things that had happened.

When they had assembled with the elders and consulted together, they gave a large sum of money to the soldiers, saying, "Tell them, 'His disciples came at night and stole Him *away* while we slept.' And if this comes to the governor's ears, we will appease him and make you secure."

So they took the money and did as they were instructed. [This is commonly reported among the Jews until this day.]

A FIRST APPEARANCE TO TWO DISCIPLES
(Cleopas and Another on the Way to Emmaus)

Now behold, two [disciples] were traveling that same day to a village called Emmaus, which was seven miles from Jerusalem. And they talked together of all these things which had happened.

So it was while they conversed and reasoned, that Jesus Himself drew near and went with them. But their eyes were restrained, so that they did not know Him.

And He said to them, "What kind of conversation *is* this that you have with one another as you walk and are sad?"

The one whose name was Cleopas answered and said to Him, "Are You the only stranger in Jerusalem, and have You not known the things which happened there in these days?"

And He said to them, "What things?"

So they said to Him, "The things concerning Jesus of Nazareth, who was a Prophet mighty in deed and word before God and all the people, and how the chief priests and our rulers delivered Him to be condemned to death, and crucified Him. But we were hoping that [He would redeem Israel.] Indeed, besides all this, today is the third day since these things happened.

"Yes, and certain women of our company, who arrived at the tomb early, astonished us. When they did not find His body, they came saying that they had also seen a vision of angels who said He was alive. And certain of those *who were* with us went to the tomb and found *it* just as the women had said; but Him they did not see."

Then He said to them, "O foolish ones, and slow of heart to believe in all that the prophets have spoken! Ought not the Christ to have suffered these things and to enter into His glory?"

And beginning at Moses and all the Prophets, [Jesus] expounded to them in all the Scriptures the things concerning Himself.

Then they drew near to the village where they were going, and He indicated that He would have gone farther. But they constrained Him, saying, "Abide with us, for it is toward evening, and the day is far spent."

And He went in to stay with them.

Now it came to pass, as He sat at the table with

them, that He took bread, blessed and broke *it,* and gave it to them. Then their eyes were opened and they knew Him; and He vanished from their sight.

And they said to one another, "Did not our heart burn within us while He talked with us on the road, and while He opened the Scriptures to us?"

THE REPORT OF THE TWO DISCIPLES

So [the two disciples] rose up that very hour and returned to Jerusalem, and they found the eleven and those *who were* with them gathered together, saying, "The Lord is risen indeed . . . And they told about the things *that had happened* on the road, and how He was known to them in the breaking of bread.

THE FIRST APPEARANCE TO A GROUP

Then, the same day at evening, being the first *day* of the week, when the doors were shut where the disciples were assembled, for fear of the Jews, Jesus came and stood in the midst, and said to them, "Peace *be* with you." When He had said this, He showed them *His* hands, His side, [and His feet].

And He said to them, "Why are you troubled? And why do doubts arise in your hearts? [It is I

Myself. Handle Me and see, for a spirit does not have flesh and bones as you see I have]."

But while they still did not believe for joy, and [wondered], He said to them, "Have you any food here?" So they gave Him a piece of a broiled fish and some honeycomb.

So Jesus said to them again, "Peace to you! As the Father has sent Me, I also send you." And when He had said this, He breathed on *them,* and said to them, "Receive the Holy Spirit. If you forgive the sins of any, they are forgiven them; if you retain the *sins* of any, they are retained."

Now Thomas, called the Twin, one of the twelve, was not with them when Jesus came. The other disciples therefore said to him, "We have seen the Lord."

So he said to them, "Unless I see in His hands the print of the nails, and put my finger into the print of the nails, and put my hand into His side, I will not believe."

THE APPEARANCE TO DOUBTING THOMAS

And after eight days His disciples were again inside, and Thomas with them.

Jesus came, the doors being shut, and stood in the midst, and said, "Peace to you!" Then He said to Thomas, "Reach your finger here, and look at My hands; and reach your hand *here,* and put *it* into My side. Do not be unbelieving, but believing."

And Thomas answered and said to Him, "My Lord and my God!"

Jesus said to him, "Thomas, because you have seen Me, you have believed. Blessed *are* those who have not seen and *yet* have believed."

And truly Jesus did many other signs in the presence of His disciples, which are not written in this book; but these are written that you may believe that Jesus is the Christ, the Son of God, and that believing you may have life in His name.

THE APPEARANCE TO SEVEN BESIDE THE SEA

After these things Jesus showed Himself again to the disciples at the Sea of Tiberias, and in this way He showed *Himself:*

Simon Peter, Thomas called the Twin, Nathanael of Cana in Galilee, the *sons* of Zebedee, and two others of His disciples were together. Simon Peter said to them, "I am going fishing."

They said to him, "We are going with you also."

They went out and immediately got into the boat, and that night they caught nothing. But when the morning had now come, Jesus stood on the shore; yet the disciples did not know that it was Jesus. Then Jesus said to them, "Children, have you any food?"

They answered Him, "No."

And He said to them, "Cast the net on the right side of the boat, and you will find *some*." So they cast, and now they were not able to draw it in because of the multitude of fish.

Therefore that disciple whom Jesus loved [the disciple John] said to Peter, "It is the Lord!"

PETER'S EXCITEMENT

Now when Simon Peter heard that it was the Lord, he put on *his* outer garment (for he had removed it), and plunged into the sea. But the other disciples came in the little boat (for they were not far from land, but about two hundred cubits), dragging the net with fish. Then, as soon as they had come to land, they saw a fire of coals there, and fish laid on it, and bread.

Jesus said to them, "Bring some of the fish which you have just caught."

Simon Peter went up and dragged the net to land, full of large fish, one hundred and fifty-three; and although there were so many, the net was not broken. Jesus said to them, "Come *and* eat breakfast." Yet none of the disciples dared ask Him, "Who are You?"—knowing that it was the Lord.

Jesus then came and took the bread and gave it to them, and likewise the fish.

This *is* now the third time Jesus showed Himself to His disciples after He was raised from the dead.

So when they had eaten breakfast, Jesus said to Simon Peter, "Simon, *son* of Jonah, do you love Me more than these?"

He said to Him, "Yes, Lord; You know that I love You."

[Jesus] said to him, "Feed My lambs."

He said to him again a second time, "Simon, *son* of Jonah, do you love Me?"

He said to Him, "Yes, Lord; You know that I love You."

[Jesus] said to him, "Tend My sheep."

He said to him the third time, "Simon, *son* of Jonah, do you love Me?"

Peter was grieved because He said to him the third time, "Do you love Me?"

And he said to Him, "Lord, You know all things; You know that I love You."

Jesus said to him, "Feed My sheep."

JESUS TELLS OF PETER'S LATER SUFFERING

"[Truly, truly], I say to you, when you were younger, you girded yourself and walked where you wished; but when you are old, you will stretch out your hands, and another will gird you and carry *you* where you do not wish."

This He spoke, signifying by what death he would glorify God. And when He had spoken this, He said to him, "Follow Me."

Then Peter, turning around, saw the disciple

whom Jesus loved following, who also had leaned on His breast at the supper, and said, "Lord, who is the one who betrays You?" Peter, seeing him, said to Jesus, "But Lord, what *about* this man?"

Jesus said to him, "If I will that he remain till I come, what *is that* to you? You follow Me."

Then this saying went out among the brethren that this disciple would not die. Yet Jesus did not say to him that he would not die, but, "If I will that he remain till I come, what *is that* to you?"

This is the disciple who testifies of these things, and wrote these things; and we know that his testimony is true.

And there are also many other things that Jesus did, which if they were written one by one, I suppose that even the world itself could not contain the books that would be written.

OTHER APPEARANCE OF JESUS

Then the eleven disciples went away into Galilee, to the mountain which Jesus had appointed for them. When they saw Him, they worshiped Him; but some doubted.

THE GREAT COMMISSION

And Jesus came and spoke to them, saying, "All authority has been given to Me in heaven and on earth. Go therefore and make disciples of all the nations, baptizing them in the name of the Father and of the Son and of the Holy Spirit, teaching them to observe all things that I have commanded you; and lo, I am with you always, *even* to the end of the age."

A BRIEF SUMMARY AND INSTRUCTIONS

Then He said to them, "These *are* the words which I spoke to you while I was still with you, that all things must be fulfilled which were written in the Law of Moses and *the* Prophets and *the* Psalms concerning Me." And He opened their understanding, that they might comprehend the Scriptures.

"Thus it is written, and thus it was necessary for the Christ to suffer and to rise from the dead the third day, and that repentance and remission of sins should be preached in His name to all nations, beginning at Jerusalem.

"And you are witnesses of these things. Behold, I send the Promise of My Father upon you; but tarry in the city of Jerusalem until you are endued with power from on high."

THE APPEARANCE AND THE ASCENSION

And He led them out as far as Bethany, and He lifted up His hands and blessed them. Now it came to pass, while He blessed them, that He was parted from them. [A cloud received Him out of their sight and carried Him up into heaven].

And while they watched and looked steadfastly toward heaven, behold, two men stood by them in white apparel, who also said, "Men of Galilee, why do you stand gazing up into heaven? This *same* Jesus, who was taken up from you into heaven, will so come in like manner as you saw Him go into heaven."

Then they returned to Jerusalem from the mount called Olivet, which is near Jerusalem, a Sabbath day's journey.

LUKE'S LATER WORDS

[Jesus] also presented Himself alive after His suffering by many infallible proofs, being seen by them during forty days and speaking of the things pertaining to the kingdom of God.

And being assembled together with *them,* Jesus commanded them not to depart from Jerusalem, but to wait for the Promise of the Father, "which," *He said,* "you have heard from Me; for John truly baptized with water, but you shall be baptized with the Holy Spirit not many days from now."

[The disciples] asked Him, "Lord, will You at this time restore the kingdom to Israel?"

And He said to them, "It is not for you to know times or seasons which the Father has put in His own authority. But you shall receive power when the Holy Spirit has come upon you; and you shall be witnesses to Me in Jerusalem, and in all Judea and Samaria, and to the end of the earth."[2]

JESUS' APPEARANCE TO PAUL

[After His ascension Jesus appeared to the Apostle Paul on the road to Damascus.]

Suddenly a light shone around him from heaven. [Paul] fell to the ground, and heard a voice saying to him, "Saul, Saul, why are you persecuting Me?"

And Paul asked, "Who are You, Lord?"

Then the Lord said, "I am Jesus, whom you are persecuting. It *is* hard for you to kick against the goads."

[Paul], trembling and astonished, said, "Lord, what do You want me to do?"

Then the Lord *said* to him, "Arise and go into the city, and you will be told what you must do."[3]

The Apostle Paul stated that before His ascension, Jesus was seen by over five hundred brethren at one time, of whom, Paul said the greater part remained to his day. Paul also said that he was seen by Jesus' brother, James. And Paul also said, "Then last of all, He was seen by me" (1 Corinthians 15:6–8).

JESUS' APPEARANCE TO JOHN

[Out on an island in the Aegean Sea, Jesus appeared to the Apostle John and revealed Himself to him.]

"I was in the Spirit on the Lord's Day, and I heard behind me a loud voice, as of a trumpet, saying, 'I am the Alpha and the Omega, the First and the Last,' and, 'What you see, write in a book and send *it* to the seven churches which are in Asia.' Then [John] turned to see the voice that spoke [to him].

[And John said,] "I saw *One* like the Son of Man, clothed with a garment down to the feet and girded about the chest with a golden band. His head and hair *were* white like wool, as white as snow, and His eyes like a flame of fire; His feet *were* like fine brass, as if refined in a furnace, and His voice as the sound of many waters; He had in His right hand seven stars, out of His mouth went a sharp two-edged sword, and His countenance *was* like the sun shining in its strength. And when I saw Him, I fell at His feet as dead.

"But He laid His right hand on me, saying to me, 'Do not be afraid; I am the First and the Last. I *am* He who lives, and was dead, and behold, I am alive forevermore. And I have the keys of Hades and of Death. Write the things which you have seen, and the things which are, and the things which will take place after this'" (Revelation 1:9–19).

[After Jesus revealed to John His future program for His followers and the World, John said:] "Even so, come, Lord Jesus!" (Revelation 22:20).

THE RESULTS OF THESE APPEARANCES

Ever since the appearances of Jesus in those early days after His resurrection and after His ascension, His followers have been telling the story of Jesus throughout the world to everyone. They tell the story, not just because they were told to tell it. They tell the story of Jesus because it is the greatest and sweetest story ever told.

TRIBUTES OF JESUS' ENEMIES

ONE WOULD EXPECT the friends of another to pay tribute to the person they love and respect. For example, John the Baptist said of Jesus, "He is the Lamb that takes away the sin of the world." Peter, when asked, "What do you think of Jesus?" answered, "He is the Christ, the Son of the Living God!" Even doubting Thomas said of Jesus, "My Lord and my God!"

However, the enemies of Jesus paid Him some of the highest tributes:

The Pharisees were bitter enemies of Jesus. They did everything possible to oppose and destroy the reputation of Jesus. They wrapped together their animosity and hatred in one grand slam pitch and hurled it at Jesus: *"This Man is a friend of sinners!"* What a tribute!

Pilate, the very ruler who sentenced Jesus to be crucified talked with Jesus, and he tried to bypass the cross. But for fear of the crowd, he followed their demands. But Pilate openly stated, *"I find no fault in this Man!"*

Judas, the one who betrayed Jesus for thirty pieces of silver, followed Jesus for three long years.

He watched every move Jesus made. He knew Jesus. And after he betrayed Jesus, he made this open statement to the authorities, *"I have betrayed innocent blood!"*

"And you, *Centurion and soldiers,* who led Jesus to the cross and nailed Him to that tree, what have you to say about Jesus?" They answered, *"Truly, this was the Son of God!"*

If the enemies of Jesus had accepted Him according to their tributes to Him, they would have received eternal life and His eternal kingdom at His first advent.

Yes, some of the highest tributes paid to Jesus were paid to Him by His enemies!

CHRIST'S PASSION BRINGS
GOOD NEWS

*"Go into the all the World and proclaim the
Good News to everyone!"*
(MARK 14:15)

SOME PEOPLE THINK that the Bible is just a book about religion and rules. They believe that, if there is a God, He only wants to control us so that we can't fully enjoy life. Such is the deception of God's adversary, Satan, the accuser of man. Satan seeks our destruction.

The story of Jesus began before the foundation of the world, and became a reality because we are God's prize creation. He desires that we live abundantly and eternally with Him. Even though we have turned away from Him, He wants to forgive and restore us to the position He intended for us when He created the first man and woman, Adam and Eve.

The Bible presents the *Good News* (*gospel*) of how God has made available a *new beginning* for all of us.

Most of the news we hear is bad news. Therefore, we consider it a joy to share some *GOOD NEWS* with you.

A SERIOUS REALIZATION
CAN CHANGE ONE'S LIFE

A certain young man wanted to be an entertainer—sing and play the guitar. That dream kept him going in his earlier years. However, at times, he became disenchanted, realizing how quickly well-known entertainers pass from the scene. Then, he realized that all of us pass from this life at some time. And after some serious thinking, he decided that anything he would do of eternal value would have to be something he was doing for God.

He is now happy to tell everyone that this is what keeps him going today—*knowing that if he died tonight, he still would be with God, still involved in His eternal program!*

EVERY PERSON'S GREATEST NEED

Being accepted by God and being involved in His eternal program is every person's greatest need, and it has been the greatest quest of some. Since we were created by God to be involved in His eternal program (to have eternal life), it is only reasonable to conclude that we can never be truly satisfied until we have peace with God.

THINK ABOUT THIS QUESTION:

What do you think it takes to be accepted by God and be involved in His eternal program NOW and even after this life has ended?

When most people are asked that question, they usually begin to talk about the good things they do or need to do. Some people have related how they have searched through the different religions of the world, engaged in rituals, or have inflicted themselves with bodily pain in order to be what they thought God wanted them to be.

If our quest for inner peace and purpose is only something we hope to find, we will never be content or feel secure. Our search among religions and personal improvement will leave us empty, hopeless, and helpless. The Bible says, *"There is a way that seems right to a man, but its end is the way of death"* (Proverbs 14:12).

Here is the **Good News!**

ETERNAL LIFE
IS A FREE GIFT!

Yes, the Bible says, *"The gift of God is eternal life"* (Romans 6:23).

And, not only is eternal life a free gift, but . . .

WE CAN KNOW
THAT WE HAVE IT

Yes, we can know that we have it! The Bible says, *"These things I have written . . . that you may know that you have eternal life"* (1 John 5:13).

THE GIFT IS FREE BECAUSE
WE CAN'T EARN IT

The Bible says, *"For by Grace you have been saved through faith, and that not of yourselves,* it is *the gift of God, not of works, lest anyone should boast"* (Ephesians 2:8–9).

Some people find it difficult to accept that forgiveness from God and the resulting eternal relationship with Him is free. They think that a person can change to be acceptable to God. However, as we read the daily newspapers, listen to the radio, or watch television with reports of wars, violence, and death all around us, we should know that people do not really change.

If we deserved eternal life or could earn it, we would be bragging about our achievement. But, the standard is just too high for any of us to earn it.

The *Good News* brings us hope as individuals in a world filled with uncertainty and helps us see that God offers us a new beginning. In fact, He has taken the initiative in restoring us to Himself. This was necessary for the following reasons:

BECAUSE OF WHO WE ARE

The reason there is so much suffering and turmoil in the world is because people are at war with God. We are rebels. The Bible clearly states that we are opposed to God. In general, people have become enemies of God and an enemy to themselves and others. The word *sinner* means *missing the mark*. We have chosen to go our own way and have missed God's better way. We have decided that we do not need God and will go our own way and do our own thing.

The Bible says, *"All we like sheep have gone astray, we have turned everyone to his own way"* (Isaiah 53:6). And again, *"All have sinned and come short of the glory of God"* (Romans 3:23). Even the good things we try to do fall short of God's holy nature. We cannot make ourselves acceptable to God. Trying not to sin, sin less, or just do little sins doesn't impress God.

The Bible says, *"All our righteousnesses* are *as filthy rags"* (Isaiah 64:6 KJV). The Bible also says, *"For whoever shall keep the whole law, and yet stumble in one point, he is guilty of all"* (James 2:10).

NOT A BIG SINNER?

If we only sinned one sin a day, that would be 365 sins per year. If we live to be 70 years old, we would have 25,550 sins on our record. That is indeed a heavy load of sins to be carrying around.

If we appeared before a judge in a traffic court with 25,550 speeding tickets, what do you think the judge would say to us? We would not expect him to say, "Your driving record is okay. I'll accept it! You should be rewarded! Please, be my guest at dinner!" How absurd!

That brings us to another reason why the gift must be free:

BECAUSE OF WHO GOD IS

God is holy and righteous and cannot accept man's sinful nature or behavior. The Bible says, *"The judgments of the Lord are true and righteous altogether"* (Psalm 19:9). The Bible also says, *"For the wrath of God is revealed from heaven against all ungodliness and unrighteousness of men, who suppress the truth in unrighteousness"* (Romans 1:18).

We sometimes want to think that God, in His love, will overlook our sins and just dismiss them, but that is not the case. God cannot let sin go unpunished. God is love, but He is also just. Our God is a *holy* God! You cannot have a loving and faithful God unless He is truly righteous and just, committed to justice for all and the protection of those He loves.

The Bible says that according to God's holy law, the whole world *"has become guilty before God"* (Romans 3:19). And the Bible also says, *"The wages of sin is death"* (Romans 6:23). Death means a separation from physical life and also eternal separation from life with God. The Bible also says that man is condemned and will receive the full judgment of God.

IMPORTANT QUESTIONS

If we are sinners, but God demands holiness, how can we ever be with God again? If God can only receive those who are holy and righteous, does His free gift provide that righteousness which He expects? If our sins must be punished, settling our sin debt, does the free gift provide the full payment for our sin debt?

The answers to these questions are found in God's love for us and in His wisdom to activate that love so as to settle our sin debt and provide us the free gift of eternal life.

JESUS PAID FOR THE FREE GIFT!

The Bible says, *"For God so loved the world that He gave His only begotten Son, that whoever believes in Him should not perish but have everlasting life"* (John 3:16). God came down to us in Jesus. *"God was in Christ reconciling the world to Himself"* (2 Corinthians 5:19).

Since we cannot establish a new beginning with God because of our sins, God must provide the payment for our sin debt and provide our righteousness. And He did just that through His Son Jesus Christ. The Bible says. *"In the beginning was the Word, and the Word was with God, and the Word was God. He was in the beginning with God . . . . All things were made through*

Him. . . . In Him was life, and the life was the light of men. . . . And the Word became flesh and dwelt among us, and we beheld His glory, the glory as of the only begotten of the Father, full of grace and truth" (John 1:1–4, 14).

The Greek word *logos*, translated *word* in the above passage, denotes expression. The passage is relating how God revealed and expressed Himself to us with His personal Word, His Son, who was with Him in creation. God expressed Himself through His Son in human form. God came to express Himself in a most intimate personality. That is indeed some *Good News!*

Most world religions are about man's attempts to reach or climb up to God, but really God has come down to us to restore and establish a most personal and eternal relationship with us. And as the passage said, *"In Him [Jesus Christ] was life."*

Jesus Christ came to negotiate God's peace plan with us. He is the mediator between God and man. *"For there is one God and one Mediator between God and men, the Man Christ Jesus, who gave Himself a ransom for all."* (1 Timothy 2:5–6).

Any good mediator must be able to appreciate the situation of both parties involved in a confrontation and represent both. He must be fair with both parties and do all he possibly can to bring them together again.

Only Jesus Christ could do that. And He does it so well. Since He is truly God, He is truly holy, as God is holy. Since He is truly Man, He can relate to our situation. We can trust Jesus to work things out. Yes, we must believe He has provided all that is necessary to bring us back to God.

JESUS PAID OUR SIN DEBT

First, Jesus paid our sin debt by taking God's punishment for our sins upon Himself. The suffering of Jesus at Calvary shows just how much God hates sin and also just how much He loves us. As the perfect Mediator, Jesus satisfied God's righteous judgment by taking that punishment. The Bible says that He was *"Smitten by God, and afflicted.... He was wounded for our transgressions, He was bruised for our iniquities; the chastisement for our peace was upon Him"* (Isaiah 53:4–5).

Jesus paid for our sins and purchased our gift of eternal life. When our Lord was dying on the Cross, He said, *"It is finished!"* (John 19:30). Actually, *tetelestai*, the Greek word translated "It is finished," really means *"PAID IN FULL!"*

Next, not only did Jesus pay our sin debt while we were under sin's burden and doomed to receive the just punishment for it, He also provided us with His righteousness so that we could be with our Holy God. Jesus is as holy and righteous as His Father. He is our sinless Savior. And God transferred His Son's righteousness to us. The Bible says, *"For He [God] made Him [Jesus] who knew no sin to be sin for us, that we might become the righteousness of God in Him"* (2 Corinthians 5:21).

GOD CAN ACCEPT US IN JESUS

The free gift of eternal life is in Jesus. Jesus said, *"I am the way, the truth, and the life. No one comes to the Father except through Me"* (John 14:6).

In Jesus, we have His righteousness and eternal life with God. We have a new position with God in Christ. If we will accept God's Son, God will declare us to be in His Son. God will accept us in Jesus and see us just as righteous as Jesus. We become the righteousness of God in our new position in Christ:

"Therefore, if anyone is in Christ, he is a new creation; old things have passed away; behold, all things have become new" (2 Corinthians 5:17).

God has truly demonstrated the acceptance of His Son's sacrifice by raising Him from the dead! (John 20). Jesus is alive and we can be alive in Him.

THE GIFT MUST BE RECEIVED

God is not going to force His gift upon us, but there is no doubt as to how we can have it.

We receive the free gift by *"repentance toward God and faith toward our Lord Jesus Christ"* (Acts

20:21). It is really *Good News* to know that we don't have to wonder or guess about what it takes to have peace with God, eternal life, and knowledge that everything is okay between God and us. God has made it very clear as to how we can have the free gift of eternal life.

WE MUST HAVE A MIND CHANGE
ABOUT OUR SINS

God takes the initiative in helping us repent. The Bible says, *"For godly sorrow produces repentance leading to salvation, not to be regretted; but the sorrow of the world produces death"* (2 Corinthians 7:10).

If we are just sorry for our sins because we were caught or suffered some personal loss, that is not repentance toward God. Such thinking doesn't change character but leaves us under God's condemnation. But when our sorrow for sin is according to the will of God, that sorrow can produce a change of mind about sin.

The word repentance means a *"change of mind."* It means that we begin to see sin and rebellion as God sees it. We begin to realize that our sin hurts us and others, and that it separates us from God. Repentance means that we begin to feel bad, as God does, about our sins, and we wish we had never sinned.

Repentance means that we desire to be rid of

sin and that we have a desire to live our lives with Jesus and for God.

Repentance is not sinlessness. We can never be sinless in this life. We are accepted by God in Christ's righteousness.

However, repentance is a mind-set which motivates us to confess the sin revealed to us and seek God's help so that we can be transformed into the likeness of Jesus.

Repentance is a change of mind which helps us to recognize sin, realize its danger, and remove ourselves from its temptation.

WE MUST TRUST JESUS CHRIST ALONE

We can receive God's free gift of eternal life, by believing and accepting Jesus Christ. We must *trust Jesus Christ alone* as our way back to God.

Saving faith is not just an intellectual understanding of facts about Jesus. We can believe Jesus is the Son of God and Savior of the world and still not receive Him as our personal Savior and Lord.

The demons of Satan believe in Jesus intellectually. The Bible says, *"You believe that there is one God. You do well. Even the demons believe; and tremble"* (James 2:19).

The demons know that there is one God and they know that Jesus is His Son. They even tremble at His power, but they do not desire to think or act like Him.

Saving faith is not just believing that Jesus lived and died and even rose again as we believe that George Washington lived and died and was the first president of the United States. Saving faith is committing ourselves totally to Jesus for all we need.

We can look at a sturdy chair in the living room of our house and admire its strength and ability to support anyone who sits in it. In fact, we have witnessed its ability to support those who have sat in it.

But until we personally trust the weight of **our** body to that chair, it will not actually support us. Just so, *unless we cast ourselves upon Jesus completely, He cannot really support us. If we want God's free gift, we must receive Jesus as our Savior.*

> *"As many as received Him, to them He gave the right (power) to become children of God"* (JOHN 1:12).

> *"Therefore, being justified by faith, we have peace with God through our Lord Jesus Christ"* (ROMANS 5:1).

THE SAILOR WITHOUT A SHIP

An old sailor on his death bed, uncertain of his standing with God, was expressing fear of dying.

A young preacher at his bedside kept saying, "Believe on Jesus! Have faith in Him."

The old sailor responded, "I've been hearing that all my life, but I need something to bear me up."

The preacher said, "Old sailor, let us suppose that while out at sea, a storm tore your ship apart. You were overboard with no land in sight, struggling to save yourself. You realized that soon it would all be over. Suddenly! A large piece of the old ship came floating near you. What would you do?"

The old sailor replied, "I'd cast myself upon that old piece of the ship so it would bear me up."

The young preacher replied, "Jesus is near you right now, and you must cast yourself upon Him. He will bear you up."

The old sailor's last words were, "He's bearing me up, Yes, He's bearing me up!"

Having faith and believing in Jesus is the act of casting ourselves upon Him, fully trusting in what He did to pay the price for our sins and bear us up to God

We may never cast ourselves upon Jesus unless we are convicted that our condition is as that of the old sailor, hopeless and helpless.

When we truly understand our condition and have a change of mind under God's conviction and cast ourselves upon Jesus, He will bear us up to God.

WE CAN RECEIVE THE
FREE GIFT RIGHT NOW!

It is indeed *Good News* to know that we don't have to wait until we die to have eternal life. We can receive God's free gift this very moment. Jesus is saying to you:

> *"Behold, I stand at the door and knock. If anyone hears my voice and opens the door, I will come in"* (REVELATION 3:20).

Would you like to receive Jesus right now? If so, you can pray a prayer like this:

> "Dear Lord Jesus, I know that I'm a sinner.
> I know that I cannot save myself.
> Jesus, I believe you died for me.
> I believe You were raised from the dead.
> I believe you will live *With* and *In* me forever.
> Forgive me of my sins and come into my heart and life.
> Thank you, Lord for loving me.
> Thank You for Your free gift of eternal life, Amen."

If you prayed as sincerely as you know how, you can be assured that God and Jesus heard you. And there is joy in heaven. *"I say to you that likewise there will be more joy in heaven over one sinner who repents than over ninety-nine just persons who need no repentance"* (Luke 15:7).

Prophecies of Jesus' Resurrection, Ascension, and Second Coming

PSALMS 16:10.
"For You will not leave my soul in Sheol, nor will You allow Your Holy One to see corruption."

PSALMS 24:7.
"Lift up your heads, O you gates! And be lifted up, you everlasting doors! And the King of glory shall come in."

PSALMS 68:18.
"You have ascended on high, You have led captivity captive."

PSALMS 97:9.
"For You, LORD, *are* most high above all the earth; You are exalted far above all gods."

HOSEA 6:2.
"On the third day He will raise us up, That we may live in His sight."

PSALMS 110:1.
"The LORD said to my Lord, 'Sit at My right hand, Till I make Your enemies Your footstool.'"

JOEL 2:28.
"And it shall come to pass afterward, that I will pour out My Spirit on all flesh; Your sons and your daughters shall prophesy, Your old men shall dream dreams, Your young men shall see visions."

ACTS 2:33.
"Therefore being exalted to the right hand of God, and having received from the Father the promise of the Holy Spirit, He poured out this which you now see and hear."

HEBREWS 7:25.
"Therefore He is also able to save to the uttermost those who come to God through Him, since He always lives to make intercession for them."

HEBREWS 9:24–28.
"For Christ has not entered the holy places made with hands, *which are* copies of the true, but into heaven itself, now to appear in the presence of God for us . . . . To those who eagerly wait for Him He will appear a second time, apart from sin, for salvation."

ZECHARIAH 14:1–4.
"In that day His feet will stand on the Mount of Olives, which faces Jerusalem on the east."

REVELATION 11:15.
"Then the seventh angel sounded: And there were loud voices in heaven, saying, 'The kingdoms of this world have become *the kingdoms* of our Lord and of His Christ, and He shall reign forever and ever!'"

THE ROBES JESUS WORE

MUCH SPECULATION centers around the clothing Jesus wore on the day of His crucifixion. Some have said that the robe He wore had magical powers as was portrayed by the movie, *The Robe*. Such speculation comes from a lack of Bible study. Just what were the garments that Jesus wore on the day of His crucifixion?

The first mention of a robe was in connection with Jesus' encounter before Herod Antipas (Luke 23:6–11). Here it is said that they put a "gorgeous robe" on Him and mocked Him.

Back before Pilate, Jesus was subjected to more mocking by the soldiers. Matthew says that they put a "scarlet" robe on Jesus (Matthew 27:27–28). However, Mark and John state that the robe was purple (Mark 15:17; John 19:2). Purple was the color of royalty and better describes the mockery. Did the soldiers use the closest thing to royalty available, a scarlet robe?

It is more probable that the robe they put on Jesus was one woven or dyed of both colors, purple and scarlet. Curtains, robes, and other garments were woven or dyed to contain more than one color, and scarlet and purple were predominate (Exodus 26:1; 39:1–2, 24; see also Revelation 17:4).

Matthew may have been more inclined to notice the scarlet colors, especially with the blood of Jesus then covering the total garment. Therefore, he sees the garment as predominately scarlet. Yet, the other writers describe the actual cloth of the garment which may have been predominately purple.

Did Jesus wear more than one robe while with Pilate? This is not necessary to understand the different colors. But it is possible that the "gorgeous robe" Herod placed on Jesus is the same robe He wore at Pilate's exhibition, though it could have been removed and replaced between the different stated events.

When they took Jesus to Golgotha, they removed the robe and put His own clothes on Him (Matthew 27:31). And before they nailed Jesus to the cross, soldiers took off His garments, divided them into four parts among themselves and cast lots for them. *His* coat (tunic) was without seam, woven from the top throughout. This act was a fulfillment of prophecy (John 19:23–24; Psalm 22:18).[1]

LIST OF SCRIPTURES USED IN BEYOND HIS PASSION

THE LAST WEEK OF JESUS' MINISTRY AND THE CROSS

Arrival at Bethany, Near Jerusalem: John 11:55–57; 12:1, 9–11; Matthew 21:1–9; Luke 19:37–44; Matthew 21:10-11, 14–17 (cf. Mark 11:1–11; Luke 19:29–44; John 12:12–19)

Fig Tree Cursed; Second Cleansing of the Temple: Mark 11:12–18 (cf. Matthew 21:18–19, 12–13; Luke 19:45–48)

Discussion of Suffering and Glory: John 12:20-50

The Fig Tree Withered: Mark 11:19–25 (cf. Matthew 21:19–22; Luke 21:37–38)

The Rulers (Sanhedrin) Challenge Jesus: Matthew 21:23–46; 22:1–14 (cf. Mark 11:27–12:12; Luke 20:1–19)

Pharisees and Herodians Try to Ensnare Jesus: Matthew 22:15–22 (cf. Mark 12:13–17; Luke 20:20-26)

Puzzling Question About the Resurrection: Matthew 22:23–33 (cf. Mark 12:18–27; Luke 20:27–40)

Jesus Answers Legal Questions: Mark 12:28–34 (cf. Matthew 22:34–40)

Jesus Discusses Descent from David: Matthew 22:41–46 (cf. Mark 12:35–37; Luke 20:41–44)

Last Public Discourse and Solemn Denouncement of the Scribes and Pharisees: Matthew 23:1–39 (cf. Mark 12:38–40; Luke 20:45–47)

Observing Contributions: Mark 12: 41–44 (cf. Luke 21:1–4)

On the Mount of Olives: Matthew 24:1–51; 25:1–46 (cf. Mark 13:1–37; Luke 21:5–36)

Jesus Predicts Crucifixion: Matthew 26:1–5 (cf. Mark 14:1–2; Luke 22:1–2)

In the House of Simon the Leper, Mary of Bethany Anoints Jesus for His Burial: Matthew 26:6; John 12:2–8; Matthew 26:13 (cf. Mark 14:8–9; Matthew 26:6–13; John 12:2–8)

Judas Stung by Rebuke, Bargains to Betray Jesus: Luke 22:3–4; Matthew 26:15–16 (cf. Mark 14:10-11; Matthew 26:14–16; Luke 22:3–6)

Jesus Prepares for the Passover Meal: Luke 22:7–13 (cf. Mark 14:12–16; Matthew 26:17–19)

Jesus Partakes of Meal with Apostles: Luke 22:14–16, 24–30 (cf. Mark 14:17; Matthew 26:20)

Jesus Washes Feet of His Disciples: John 13:1–20

Jesus Points Out Judas as the Betrayer: Mark 14:18–21; John 13:23–26; Matthew 26:25; John 13:27–30 (cf. Mark 14:18–21; Matthew 26:21–25; Luke 22:21–23; John 13:21–30)

Judas Departs, Warning Against Desertion: John 13:31–38; Luke 22:35–38 (cf. John 13:31–38; Mark 14:27–31; Matthew 26:31–35; Luke 22:31–38)

Jesus Institutes Memorial Supper: Luke 22:17–20; Matthew 26:29 (cf. Luke 22:17–20; Mark 14:22–25; Matthew 26:26–29; 1 Corinthians 11:23–26)

Farewell Discourse to Disciples: John 14:1–31

Discourse on the Way to Gethsemane: John 15:1–27; 16:1–33

Christ's Intercessory Prayer: John 17:1–26

Gethsemane-Jesus in Agony: Matthew 26:30; John 18:1; Matthew 26:36–46 (cf. Mark 14:26, 32–43; Luke 22:39–46; John 18:1)

Betrayed, Arrested, and Forsaken: John 18:2–9; Matthew 26:48–50; John 18:10-11; Matthew 26:53–56; Mark 14:51–52 (cf. Mark 14:43–52; Matthew 26:47–56; Luke 22:47–53; John 18:2–12)

Jesus Examined by Annas, the Ex-High Priest: John 18:12–14, 19–23

Jesus Hurriedly Tried and Condemned by Caiaphas and the Sanhedrin, who Mock Him: Matthew 26:57, 59–68 (cf. Mark 14:53, 55–65; Luke 22:54, 63–65; John 18:24)

Peter Denies His Lord: John 18:15–18; Matthew 26:69–75; (cf. Mark 14:54, 66–72; Matthew 26:58, 66–75; Luke 22:54–62; John 18:15–18, 25–27)

After Dawn-Jesus Formally Condemned: Luke 22:66–71; (cf. Mark 15:1; Matthew 27:1)

Remorse and Suicide of Judas: Matthew 27:3–10 (cf. Acts 1:18–19)

First Time Before Pilate: John 18:28–30; Luke 23:2; John 18:31–38; Matthew 27:12–14; Luke 23:5 (cf. Mark 15:1–5; Matthew 27:2, 11–14; Luke 23:1–5; John 18:28–38)

Jesus Before Herod: Luke 23:6–12

Second Time with Pilate: Mark 15:6–8; Luke 23:13–15; Matthew 27:17–21; Luke 23:18–19; John 19:1–15; Matthew 27:24–26 (cf. Mark 15:6–15; Matthew 27:15–56; Luke 23:12–25; John 18:29—19:16)

Soldiers Mock Jesus: Matthew 27:27–30 (cf. Mark 15:16–19)

Jesus on the Way to the Cross: Mark 15:20-21; Luke 23:27–32; Matthew 27:33–34 (cf. Mark 15:20–23; Matthew 27:31–34; Luke 23:33; John 19:16–17)

The First Three Hours on the Cross: Luke 23:33–34a; John 19:23–24, 19–22; Matthew 27:39–44; Luke 23:39–43; John 19:25–27 (cf. Mark 15:24–32; Matthew 27:35–44; Luke 23:33–43; John 19:18–27)

Three Hours of Darkness (12 Noon to 3 P.M.): Matthew 27:45–49; John 19:28–30; Luke 23:46 (cf. Mark 15:33–37; Matthew 27:45–50; Luke 23:44–46; John 19:28–30)

Phenomena Accompanying Christ's Death: Matthew 27:51–56 (cf. Mark 15:38–41; Luke 23:45–49)

Burial of Jesus: John 19:31–42 (cf. Mark 15:42–46; Matthew 27:57–60; Luke 23:50-54; John 19:31–42)

The Watch of the Women at the Tomb of Jesus: Luke 23:55–56; Matthew 27:62–66 (cf. Mark 15:47; Matthew 27:61–66; Luke 23:55–56)

RESURRECTION AND ASCENSION OF JESUS CHRIST

Action of Angel Before Women Arrive, Fright of the Roman Watchers: Matthew 28:2–4

Women Going to Tomb: Mark 16:1 (cf. Matthew 28:1)

Women Approach Tomb About Sunrise on Sunday Morning. Mary Magdalene Discovery and Report to Peter and John: John 20:1–2

The Arrival of the Other Women, Their Report to the Eleven Disciples: Luke 24:1–11 (cf. Mark 16:2–8; Matthew 28:5–8)

Peter and John Visit Tomb: John 20:3–10 (cf. Luke 24:12)

Mary Magdalene's Return to the Tomb, First Appearance of the Risen Jesus: John 20:11–18 (cf. Mark 16:9–11)

Appearance of Jesus to Other Women, a Message for Jesus' Brothers: Matthew 28:9–10

Guard Report to the Jewish Rulers, Who Bribe the Guard to Tell Falsehood: Matthew 28:11–15

Appearance to Two Disciples (Cleopas and Another) on the Way to Emmaus: Luke 24:13–32 (cf. Mark 16:12–13)

Report of the Two Disciples, News of Jesus' Appearance to Simon Peter: Luke 24:33–35

Appearance to the Astonished Disciples (Thomas Absent): John 20:19–20a; Luke 24:38–43; John 20:20b-25 (cf. Mark 16:14; Luke 24:36–43; John 20:19–25)

Appearance to Disciples Next Sunday, Thomas Convinced: John 20:26–31

Appearance to Seven Disciples Beside the Sea: John 21

Appearance to About Five Hundred on Mountain in Galilee, the Great Commission: Matthew 28:16–20 (cf. Mark 16:15–18; 1 Corinthians 15:6)

Appearance to James the Brother of Jesus: 1 Corinthians 15:7

Appearance of Jesus with Another Commission: Luke 24:44–49; Acts 1:3–8 (cf. Acts 1:3–8)

Last Appearance and Ascension: Luke 24:50-51; Acts 1:9–12 (cf. Luke 24:50-53; Mark 16:19–20; Acts 1:9–12)

NOTES

THE LAST WEEK OF JESUS' MINISTRY AND THE CROSS

1. When Jesus rode the colt, the mother donkey naturally went along. Jesus may have rode each animal part of the distance.

2. Psalm 118:26. Hosanna, from the Hebrew *hosi ah na*, meaning "save us we pray."

3. Psalm 8:2.

4. While it was not the season for full fruit on a fig tree, the early green buds were food for local peasants. But the lack of buds on this fig tree indicated that it would produce no fruit that year.

5. Isaiah 56:7; Jeremiah 7:11.

6. All were given wedding garments. The one who came without a proper garment represents those who want to observe, but are not committed or a part of the expanded kingdom from all races and backgrounds. An individual's proper response is essential. Sorrow and pain (weeping and gnashing of teeth) comes to those who do not properly respond.

7. The Herodians were a party formed to support Herod, and rulers who could bring about the friendship of Rome and provide other advantages.

8. Genesis 17:7; 26:24; 28:21; Exodus 3:6, 15.

9. These two specific commandments are given in Deuteronomy 6:4–5; 10:12;30:6; and Leviticus 19:18, etc. The first part of the Ten Commandments relates to man's relationship to God, and the latter

commandments relate to man's relationship to man, Deuteronomy 5:6–21. The two commandments Jesus quoted are a summation of the Ten Commandments.

10. Phylacteries: strips containing Scripture passages, rolled up, placed in a box , and firmly attached on the forehead, left arm, and near the heart.

11. *Teacher, father*, and *master* are here not actual relationships, but positions some sought so as to have authority over others.

12. The generation that sees these described events of the end times.

13. Psalm 41:9.

14. These words were probably a rebuke, "Enough of this kind of talk."

15. Psalm 35:19; 69:4; 109:3–5.

16. The young man who fled is believed to be John Mark, the writer of Mark's Gospel, since he is the only one of the four writers who writes about this incident. John Franklin Carter, *A Layman's Harmony*, p. 303.

17. The council of the Hebrews developed during the Greek supremacy.

18. Jeremiah 32:6–9; Zechariah 11:12–13.

19. A Roman scourging was a severe beating so hideous that the victim usually fainted and not rarely died under it. The scourge consisted of a handle to which several cords or leather thongs were attached. These were weighted with jagged pieces of bone or metal to make the blows more painful. [See "Scourge-Scourging," *The International Standard Bible Encyclopaedia* , Vol. IV (Grand Rapids: Wm. B. Eerdmans, 1939, 1956), p. 2704 .]

20. Psalm 34:20. See also Exodus 12:46 and Numbers 9:12.
21. Zechariah 12:10.

PROPHECIES OF JESUS' RESURRECTION, ASCENSION, AND SECOND COMING

1. The Sabbath was over at about 6:00 PM. The Jews counted the day as beginning in the evening. The resurrection of Jesus occurred before daylight, but it was the first day of the week. Mark said the sun was rising when the women began to prepare to go to the tomb, or actually started, but by the time they were almost at the tomb, the sun had begun to rise.
2. Acts 1:3–12.
3. Acts 9:1–6.

THE ROBES JESUS WORE

1. Research on Robes Jesus Wore: William Barclay, *The Gospel of John Volume 2* (Philadelphia: The Westminster Press, 1955), p. 295. W. E. Vine, *Vine's Complete Expository Dictionary of Old and New Testament Words* (Nashville: Thomas Nelson Publishers, 1995), N.T., p, 106.

ABOUT THE AUTHORS

JIM and ROY GILLEY are brothers who have been active in evangelism and writing within a variety of ministries. They share an overwhelming desire to make the story of Jesus as clear and understandable as possible.

Jim is a graduate of Trinity College and studied at Trinity Theological Seminary and the Billy Graham School of Evangelism. He has been a trainer for Evangelism Explosion International and a trainer for *Faith,* an evangelistic venture of the North American Mission Board of the Southern Baptist Convention.

Roy graduated summa cum laude with a Th.D. from Trinity Theological Seminary and has been a pastor and teacher of English, history, and Bible as literature. He has been active in evangelism, research, and writing.

Both Roy and Jim call middle Tennessee home.